Foretold and Found

ancient America and predicted evidence of The Book of Mormon

B. Keith Christensen

D1447865

Statements

Geologist's statement, in part:

It is my opinion that Mr. Christensen has used the geological information available in a responsible manner.

Grant G. Pitcher, CPG

Archaeologist's statement, in part:

The consequences of Keith Christensen's research are far reaching...I recommend his work as being essential reading for all Book of Mormon of Mormon students.

Dr. Bruce W. Warren
Assistant Professor of Archaeology
and Anthropology, BYU (retired)

ISBN 978-0-9686254-2-2
Copyright © B. Keith Christensen 2007
Printed by Centaur Print Partners
Provo, Utah, USA

Preface

The Book of Mormon was first published in 1830 as Christian scripture from ancient America. There is external evidence of its authenticity but generally this has only been seen by 'Mormons.' (members of *The Church of Jesus Christ of Latter-day Saints*)

For example, the Book of Mormon was written in a way that originated in the Holy Land. This fits the Book of Mormon's claim that its founding people came from Jerusalem to settle in the Americas. Early Indian writings such as the *Popol Vuh* of Guatemala contain elements consistent with this claim. These and all other findings did not come to light until after the Book of Mormon was first published.

But evidence such as this takes study and few people have the time and inclination to look into it. The physical evidence introduced here is different, for the Book of Mormon says it would "be found" for a stated "intent." So this evidence is more direct and therefore easier to examine. Still, this takes more than just a casual reading.

Many can benefit from physical evidence in support of spiritual matters as shown by examples cited in the next few pages. And as shown later, there is a spiritual way to determine the truthfulness of the Book of Mormon in addition to the physical findings foretold.

These findings do not diminish nor threaten the worth of spiritual testimony that leads many to accept it. Rather, this evidence adds another dimension by which its truthfulness can be shown – and be a bridge to help many gain a spiritual conviction.

Since this booklet is only an introduction, not all elements of the evidence can be examined here. So some questions may go unanswered for now. Yet this is enough to see how these findings discovered by non-Mormon researchers fit the Book of Mormon.

Introduction

The authenticity of the Book of Mormon has been debated ever since it was first published in 1830. All the while it has been overlooked that it says certain evidence of itself would be found in our day. Findings that fit this prediction have now come to light.

Those who believe the Book of Mormon do so for spiritual reasons. Yet it declares it is intended for all mankind. But many have their own religious beliefs, others ignore religious ideals, and others deny there is God and question even the idea of spiritual things.

A Book of Mormon prophet shows this situation was anticipated for he tells of material evidence reserved for our day in support of its spiritual role. This is evidence that anyone can assess objectively, regardless of their spiritual or non-spiritual views.

To truly understand the implications of the evidence it needs to be fully read, not just scanned, skimmed, or spot read. There are places where it is detailed but this is consistent with the Book of Mormon being a true account. These details are presented as briefly as possible. The appendix provides information that enhances the significance of the evidence.

For some it will seem preposterous that there could be evidence to back the Book of Mormon. For most Mormons it is unnecessary. Still, it claims that certain evidence would be found, for a certain "intent."

If you have not yet read the Preface, please do so.

Ancient Findings for Modern Times

BACKGROUND: The Book of Mormon is an account of an ancient people descended from Joseph who is told of in the Bible. They were divinely led to the Americas from Jerusalem about 600 BC. It tells of their rise, decline, and fall – and its purpose for us today.

It contains teachings that clarify and substantiate the gospel of Christ in our day – a day when many reject moral values and deny the existence of God although the earth, the universe, and *The Mathematics of Probability*, refute the idea that all came about by chance. And it foretells evidence of itself that would be found today.

STARTLING CLAIM: The Book of Mormon tells of fair-skinned people living in ancient America in addition to Indians. That is, the original people it tells of were fair-skinned. They separated as *Nephites* and *Lamanites*. The Lamanites acquired a darker skin as with indigenous people already in the Americas. (see note, next page.) Often at war, the Lamanites defeated the Nephites in a final battle about 400 AD. Descendants of the Lamanites are among those now called *Indians*.

Evidence: Fig. 1 – Murals in *The Temple of the Warriors* in Chichen Itza, Mexico, painted about 1000 AD, recount Indian warfare. Some show fair-

Figure 1 from Chichen Itza murals

skinned people bound and in bondage. (Fig. 1; bound prisoner; man paddling boat for armed Indians)

They can't be European for Columbus didn't discover America until 1492. They can't be Vikings who came briefly to North America about 1000 AD for they landed thousands of miles north on the island of Newfoundland. They can't be storm ravaged Europeans adrift to America for the murals also show white warriors equipped for war.

These murals fit the Book of Mormon account of a fair-skinned people on the American continent before Columbus. So they provide evidence even before looking at the evidence foretold.

Note: The Book of Mormon says the Lamanites acquired a dark skin and it speaks of Nephites becoming dark too if they bred with the Lamanites. This implies genetics for the Lamanites to get their dark skin in the first place, by breeding with "children of the land" – that is, with people already in the Americas (Ether 2:10; 1 Nephi 17:32; 2 Nephi 5:21-23; "skin of blackness." Middle East views things in extremes; black vs. white. *Seven Pillars of Wisdom,* T.E. Lawrence. Book of Mormon people would carry this view to the Americas; *blackness* = brown in its various shades. Appendix, p. 56)

From Mesoamerica: The last Nephite prophet escaped the destruction of his people. He made the long journey from Mesoamerica with the original Book of Mormon inscribed on gold plates to present-day New York state to bury them for safe keeping until revealed there over 400 years later. (Although little known, ancient writing was inscribed on metal plates as well as clay tablets and written on scrolls.)

Early in the 1800s the Book of Mormon was revealed to a young man, Joseph Smith. By divine means he translated it as another testament of Jesus Christ, in support of the Bible, to restore His true gospel in the midst of the many ideas taught by the many churches and religions. Many have believed the Book of Mormon but many have been influenced against it, and others don't know how to regard it.

PHYSICAL FINDINGS: These findings, foretold in the Book of Mormon, are geological. It says they would be found today as shown in the following pages. But first there are factors to consider. For instance, those who question the existence of God look to science and these findings meet scientific criteria for they are tangible evidence. For those who believe in God, physical findings may seem unsuitable. If so, consider the following precedent.

EVIDENCE AND BELIEF: When Christ was crucified at Jerusalem "the earth did quake, and the rocks rent." (Matt. 27:51) The Roman centurion at the crucifixion and others "saw the earthquake" and other things such as darkness in the daytime. He took all this as a sign and exclaimed, "Truly this man was the Son of God."

Matthew 27:52-54; Mark 15:36-39; Luke 23:44-47

The Book of Mormon also tells of an earthquake in the Americas at the time of Christ's death at Jerusalem. It was much greater and testified of His divinity to the descendants of those who came from Jerusalem about 600 years before. Other phenomena attended this geologic event in the Americas – darkness, wind, and lightning.

We now find that non-Mormon historians, geologists, and archaeologists, have discovered that "about the time of Christ" a great earthquake and volcanic eruptions devastated Mexico and Central America. (Mesoamerica) The approximate date of the event as determined by these researchers accommodates the precise time of the event told in the Book of Mormon.

As the earthquake at Jerusalem testified to the centurion – and the geologic upheaval in ancient America testified to the people of the Book of Mormon – evidence of this event now found on the American continent testifies to us today. This evidence is extensive and well documented. Yet some could wonder if this evidence is only coincidence. So consider the following.

These discoveries fit the event in the Book of Mormon in ways and detail that would exclude even the possibility of coincidence! Also, the following dates show these findings could hardly be coincidence and thereby show the Book of Mormon is on very solid ground.

     1830 - Book of Mormon first published
     1868 - Start of geologic study in Mesoamerica
     1950 - First significant findings of the geologic event

Only divine foreknowledge could tell of this ancient calamity and in 1830 foretell future findings regarding it. If the Book of Mormon was a fraud by Joseph Smith or anyone else in his day – geologic findings today would uncover this and discredit it. Instead, the findings solidly support the Book of Mormon beyond any reasonable doubt. This is particularly seen in the high degree of agreement between details in the Book of Mormon and the findings.

It may seem extreme that evidence is called for by the Book of Mormon, but as we will see, it insists that this evidence would be found. Some may think that later findings could undermine what has been found. But the findings are well established. And "facts are facts."

In addition to this evidence, the Book of Mormon also tells of a spiritual way to know it is true. This is outlined later. But to test it spiritually it must be read with an open mind.

It is hoped that the findings shown here will give you reason to read the Book of Mormon. The history it tells, with real-life characters both good and bad, is intriguing. But more importantly, it includes spiritual insights, testifies of the divinity of Jesus Christ, and offers original gospel guidance for all mankind that was lost for centuries.

A Closer Look

This massive upheaval and evidence was foretold by the prophet Samuel the Lamanite six years before the birth of Christ. He said,

> in the day that he (Christ) shall suffer death...the earth shall shake and tremble; and the rocks...above the earth and beneath...shall be broken up...and ***shall ever after be found in seams and in cracks***....   *Helaman 14:21,22; emphasis added*

Here we see that *seams* and *cracks* or *faults* and *fissures* in modern terms, caused by this geologic event in the Americas, would *"ever after be found."* To be found "ever after" would obviously include our day when we have the science of geology.

These faults and fissures would be evidence of this event and therefore be evidence of Christ today since they came about as physical testimony of His death. And they would be evidence for the Book of Mormon since it tells of these things.

The survivors of the event of course saw the faults and fissures, but erosion and vegetation over the centuries since then would obscure them until found by geologists today.

For the Book of Mormon to be true, the faults and fissures must exist and "be found" for it says they will. This does not lessen the Book of Mormon on a spiritual level, but rather, this temporal aspect supports the spiritual as shown below.

General faults and fissures from this event are not enough, for **only major geologic changes sufficiently described in the Book of**

Mormon to make comparisons would do! These comparisons have been made and match in every detail.

That is, by comparing geologic findings with two major geologic changes told and alluded to in the Book of Mormon, and other factors, we see the event identified by researchers and the one told of in the Book of Mormon are the same one. And again, this evidence that fits the Book of Mormon account was unknown in 1830.

The intent: It was noted earlier that this evidence has *intent*. The evidence is not just a matter of interest, for the text speaks of "greater things" that have **the intent** to show

> these signs and these wonders should come to pass upon all the face of this land,
>
> to **the intent** that there should be no cause for unbelief among the children of men (regarding Christ) - And this
>
> to **the intent** that whosoever will believe might be saved...
>
> Helaman 14:28,29 parenthesis added. See Helaman 14:10

"Greater things" could not be greater earthquakes for that would obliterate the seams and cracks told of so they would not be able to "be found." Rather, the Book of Mormon says "the knowledge" that was "hid up" comprises "the greater things." (Ether 4:13) This would be the Book of Mormon itself for it was "hid up" until revealed to Joseph Smith, and tells of Christ and of the event. Mormon 5:12; 7:8

So the Book of Mormon shows that these geologic signs testify of Christ, to overcome *cause* for not believing in Him. That is, no one can say there is no evidence for the divinity of Jesus Christ. Conversely, those who *believe* (the significance of the signs) will have *cause* to believe in Him.

Of course more than these signs are needed to fully develop faith in Christ. But physical evidence can help initiate belief as with the

Roman centurion. But out of all interpretations of Christ's gospel, where can it be found in its original form?

The Book of Mormon says it has the "fulness" of the gospel, the gospel in its original form. So it follows that since the evidence it foretells actually exists, the book itself would be true and thus contain the gospel of Jesus Christ in its original form.

In addition to the centurion, there are two other biblical events that also show a role for physical evidence.

First, "many believed when they saw the miracles which he did." (John 2:23) His miracles were physical evidence which caused belief.

Second, Thomas, one of Christ's apostles, was not present when the resurrected Lord appeared to them. When Thomas heard the other apostles' account he said, "Except I shall see in his hands the print of the nails...and thrust my hand into his side, I will not believe."

John 20:25

Later Christ appeared to the apostles when Thomas was present and said to Thomas, Reach hither thy finger, and behold my hands; and reach hither thy hand, and thrust it into my side: and be not faithless, but believing. John 20:27

Christ invited Thomas to examine His wounds so he would believe. With this we learn that physical evidence is valid for fostering belief. He did not fault Thomas for wanting to see these physical signs.

John 20:29

With physical evidence persuading the centurion, the believers, and 'doubting Thomas,' the Book of Mormon is scripturally consistent in telling of physical evidence that testifies of the geologic cataclysm at Christ's death, which testifies of Him, and therefore testifies of the truth of the Book of Mormon since it tells of these things.

Secondarily, the findings show where the Book of Mormon setting was since they are in its former lands. Some have proposed maps and correlations based on theory regarding Book of Mormon lands.

In contrast, correlations shown here are from geologic evidence foretold for our day. So *this is totally different, for we have evidence specified by the Book of Mormon itself on which to base correlations*. So these would be reliable. **But the main thing is how the findings testify of the geologic event at the time of Christ's death.**

No wild coincidence can account for the detailed agreement between the findings and the Book of Mormon. These findings can help many who need physical evidence as a bridge to gain faith as shown earlier. And they can fortify many who believe but have questions or doubts.

The Findings

The Book of Mormon says that at the time of Christ's death:
> ...there arose a great storm...and terrible tempest...and the exceeding great quaking of the whole earth...And behold, the rocks were rent in twain...in seams and in cracks, upon all the face of the land.   3 Nephi 8:5-18

Modern research in Central America shows that "about the time of Christ" the southeast "Maya Highlands was devastated by a massive natural disaster."   Dr. Payson Sheets, *Ilopango Volcano and the Maya Protoclassic, 1975 field season*, Dept. of Anthropology, Univ. of Colorado, p.2

It is also described as "approximately 2,000 years ago." (Dr. Virginia Steen-McIntyre, *Ibid*, appendix, p.68) It was "a natural disaster on a large regional scale."   Sheets, *Archaeology and Volcanism in Central America*, p. 1, Univ. of Texas Press, 1983

FATE OF FOUR CITIES: The Lamanite city of Jerusalem, named after Jerusalem in the Holy Land, is included in a notable change.

> the city of Gilgal (was)...sunk, and...buried...in the depths of the earth...and the city of Onihah...and the city of Mocum ...and the city of Jerusalem...and waters have...come up in the stead thereof.
>
> 3 Nephi 9:6, 7 (edited to show the essence of what happened)

This is said in an unusual way. That is, it tells of one city sinking into the earth and the other three are added in that fate. This is like saying, "I saw John at the movies, and Tom, and Dick, and Harry." Then water came up in the *stead* of the four cities. (*stead* means "place" Webster) Water staying and not draining away indicates four lakes.

It might be thought that these cities were close together and covered by one lake since they are listed together. But all cities are listed by fate, not location. e.g. A city in the center of the land and one in the north were both destroyed by fire. (Helaman 1:27; 3 Nephi 7:12; 9:3, 9) So it follows that these four cities were apart and four lakes formed.

CORRELATION: Four lakes in Central America formed in "Recent" geologic time with collapse involved and water from subterranean sources. Names for *Jerusalem* are by one of them. The lakes are *Amatitlan* and *Atitlan* in Guatemala, and *Coatepeque* and *Ilopango* in El Salvador. (Fig. 2) United States Geol. Survey/USGS, *Bull. 1034*, 1957, p.36

The lake with names linked to *Jerusalem* is Lake Ilopango in El Salvador. It has been studied the most, by two geologists who are cited by others and by archaeologists. Their findings fit it forming "about the time of Christ." Dr. Howell Williams and Dr. Helmut Meyer-Abich, *Volcanism in the Southern Part of El Salvador* et al, Univ. of Calif., 1955

These geologists found that Lake Ilopango was created by *engulfment* (collapse) in the weathered basin of a dormant volcano. (*Ibid*)

10

(fertile soil caused by weathering in old volcanos attracted settlement in ancient times) *Collapse* and *engulfment*, with water coming from subterranean sources, echo the Book of Mormon phrasing "sunk...in the depths of the earth" with water coming "up."

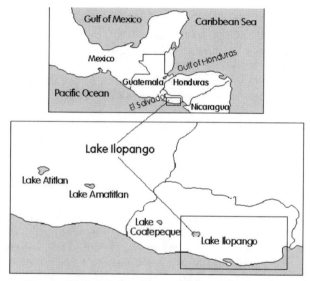

Figure 2 lakes formed by collapse and volcanism

The age of Lake Ilopango, in particular, is a specific correlation that fits the Book of Mormon account.

That is, "Ilopango, an extinct volcano [now a lake]...erupted 2,000 years ago." Sheets cited, *Science News*, v.111 Jan. 29, 1977, p. 74

Although only Lake Ilopango has been studied much, the geology of the other lakes and the moderate research there indicate they are contemporary with Lake Ilopango. e.g. Lake Atitlan's "conformation" has "extreme youth."   Rollin S. Atwood, cited in *Carnegie Institution Year Book #31,* Washington, D.C., 1932

(Research at the other lakes is about the age of the underlying rock.)

Significance: These lakes are over 2500 miles from where Joseph Smith lived, in lands he likely knew little about if at all, with origins that fit the fate of the four cities. He had only a limited frontier education when he published the Book of Mormon at age 25. Even if he knew of them, he could not know their origin as a concept to include in a fictional account for their geology was unknown in his day.

Other findings show this cataclysm was not limited to El Salvador where Lake Ilopango is located, but extended across the region we call Mesoamerica. This fits the Book of Mormon saying a great destruction took place throughout its lands, both north and south. And there is evidence that this event reached into South America.

But regardless of how far afield this geologic event extended, it took place. Again, the time of this event "about the time of Christ" as determined by geologists and archaeologists, allows for the specific time told in the Book of Mormon – when Christ died at Jerusalem.

It is important to emphasize that there is no way Joseph Smith or anyone else could know of this event in 1830. Therefore, the geologic evidence being foretold in the Book of Mormon, and this specific evidence actually being found, testify that the account in the Book of Mormon is true and thus the book is true.

Place-names: There are place-names close to Lake Ilopango that reflect Indian cultural memory of the name *Jerusalem*. These names enhance the significance of the geologic findings. Examples are in the appendix. (p. 40) But to maintain the flow of reading this main text it is suggested you go to the appendix later for this and other items.

KEY GEOLOGIC CHANGE: A *narrow* or *small* neck of land joined the main landmasses: *land northward* and *land southward*. (Alma 22:32; 63:5; Ether 10:20) The neck of land was offset west for it was in the land Bountiful which was north of a west wilderness in the land southward. (Alma 22:28-32) It is not mentioned after the cataclysm and the text shows it widened at this time, and therefore ceased to exist. (Appendix, p. 45. Again, it is suggested you go to the appendix after reading all the main text.) Locating this change offers major evidence of this event.

The Lamanite Jerusalem was in the land southward. So the neck of land would be north of Lake Ilopango since it covers this buried city.

CORRELATION: The *Motagua Fault Zone* is north of Lake Ilopango and offset west as the neck of land was. (Fig. 3) This active geologic zone is where the devastating earthquake of 1976 struck Guatemala and Guatemala City. It was lower in ancient times, allowing the sea, the Gulf of Honduras, to extend into the long V-shaped Izabal Basin that opens toward the sea. (see Fig. 3)

Therefore, from very ancient times the Motagua Fault Zone was narrower from sea to sea. Later it was elevated – in *Recent* geologic time – spilling the sea from the Izabal Basin and widening the land. (*Recent*: from appx. 50,000 BC) (USGS *Bulletin 1034*, p.7 and map) (Lake Izabal was formed by rivers flowing into the basin and flushing out the dregs of the sea left in the lowest part of the basin.)

How recent? Field study shows the Izabal Basin was unoccupied until about 2000 years ago although the land around it was occupied. More precisely, close study of the findings and the researcher's comments therein (and telephone discussion with her) indicate it was not occupied until the 1st century AD.

Dr. Barbara Voorhies, Doctoral Dissert., Yale Univ., 1969

So sea would be in the Basin until the century Christ lived and died.

13

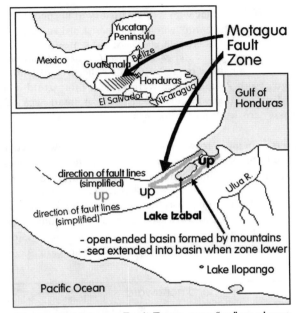

Figure 3 Motagua Fault Zone - now "up" as shown

This allows for the neck of land to be in the Motagua Fault Zone until the cataclsym told in Book of Mormon for it is north of Lake Ilopango which fits as the lake formed over the Lamanite Jerusalem.

Summary: The sea filled the Izabal Basin until the first century AD, making the Motagua Fault Zone narrower from sea to sea until then. This fits the cataclysm told in the Book of Mormon with loss of the neck of land since Christ died and resurrected in the first century AD.

GEOLOGY NOT ALONE: And there are factors such as Indian history and tradition that say there was a great natural disaster. For

14

instance, a Christian Aztec who wrote a history of his people, tells of a great upheaval of the earth "when Christ our Lord suffered."

Ixtlilxochitl, cited by Milton R. Hunter, T. S. Ferguson,
Ancient America and the Book of Mormon, p. 190

Another factor – a narrow pass – also shows the neck of land was in the Motagua Fault Zone. (There were several things told of in the Book of Mormon, that were narrow: narrow or small neck of land, narrow pass, narrow strip of wilderness. Appendix, p. 57)

Narrow pass: In the narrow neck of land was a narrow pass that "led by the sea into the land northward, yea, by the sea, on the west and on the east." It survived the cataclysm for it is mentioned afterwards.

Alma 22:32,33; 50:33,34; Mormon 3:5

CORRELATION: The only way for the pass to lead north to south and "by" the seas east and west, would be to run diagonally through the neck of land. There is a feature, the Guatemala Depression, that curves diagonally through the Motagua Fault Zone. (Fig. 4)

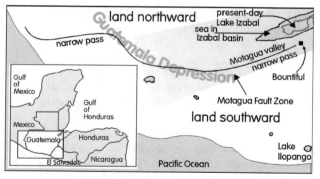

Figure 4 narrow pass

Its southern stretch is the Motagua river valley which is only a half-mile wide at its mouth. (above its flood plain) The mouth of this valley is "by" the Izabal Basin that the Gulf of Honduras extended into. To the northwest another valley branches off to run "by" the Pacific. (see Fig. 4)

Therefore, this pass in the mountainous Motagua Fault Zone would fit as the narrow pass in the narrow neck of land told of in the Book of Mormon. This enhances the geologic evidence that shows the neck of land was located here and is another physical factor that indicates authenticity of the Book of Mormon.

JESUS CHRIST AND ANCIENT AMERICA: In the King James Bible, which most Christians use, it is recorded that Jesus said,

> other sheep I have, which are not of this fold: them also I must bring, and they shall hear my voice; and there shall be **one fold**, [and] one shepherd.   John 10:16 emphasis added

This has been taken to mean that Christ's Word would go to others. But we find that it actually means He would personally visit others and the Book of Mormon records fulfilment of His statement. How can this be and how is this connected with geologic evidence? The following shows how.

The earliest scripture gives the most likely reading. (Greek) It says

> other sheep I have, which are not of this fold...and my voice they will hear; and there shall be **one flock**, one shepherd."
>
> John 10:16; from early Greek, emphasis added
> George Ricker Berry, Zondervan Publishers

The familiar King James Bible cited first says "there shall be one fold," not "one flock" as in the earlier Greek. At least seven modern translations of the Bible also say "one flock" rather than "one fold."

e.g. *Revised Standard Version, Jerusalem Bible, The Living Bible*

A *fold* is an "enclosed place" typically associated with sheep. (Webster)

For all *sheep* to be in one fold, all believers would have to be in one location, which of course would be a problem for a worldwide faith.

But in the context of *one shepherd* and *one flock*, a shepherd's flock can be divided and taken to different places as when, with the aid of helpers, he divides his flock to take advantage of better pastures in these separate places. In these separate places these segments of his flock would be gathered into separate folds.

The New Testament was originally written in Greek. The original manuscripts have been lost but early copies of the original Greek still exist. With these earliest texts as reference, it is evident that Christ was speaking of believers as one flock gathered to separate folds.

It could be considered that this fits all Christian congregations in the world but there are several factors that indicate this is not what it refers to.

That is, the *word* of God – His teachings – can be taught by His servants, but the "other sheep" were to hear His voice. The apostle Paul learned that the voice of the Lord is "the voice of his mouth." (Acts 22:14) Voice is "sound made through the mouth." (Webster) *Word* is "speech" which the voice utters (Webster) but can be written or taken to others, as *the Word of God* in the Bible. Luke 1:2

And a voice cannot be taken elsewhere unless in modern times by electronic means. Even if hard to accept the distinction between *voice* and *word*, this difference is shown in the Bible. Therefore, for *other sheep* to hear Christ's voice He would have to visit them. We may use the term *voice* at times in the sense of *word,* but Christ said *word* when it means His message and not necessarily His voice.

e.g. Matthew 13:19; Mark 7:13; John 5:24

In the New Testament the only cases where His voice does not mean personal contact are those involving the Holy Spirit. (Heb. 3:7; 12:19; John 18:37) Still, He tells of visiting *other sheep* of another fold. So these people would be in a place other than the *fold* of Jerusalem-/Judea where He made the statement in the Bible.

This cannot be construed to refer to His second coming since "this fold" of Jerusalem where He made the statement is where He will initiate His second coming. (Zechariah 14:1-4) So His visit to those who "are not of this fold" would involve another time and place.

For others to hear His voice He would need to visit them in person. But when and where? His visit to "other sheep" is linked to the geologic event told in the Book of Mormon, and the event itself and the visit of Jesus Christ to these "other sheep" echoes a geologic event and visit of deity told of in Indian history.

Fulfilment recorded in the Book of Mormon: The geologic event at the time of Christ's crucifixion testified of His death to the posterity of those who came from Jerusalem to the Americas almost 600 years before. Then, after His resurrection, in fulfilment of His statement about "other sheep," He visited those who survived the geologic event in the Americas. 3 Nephi 15:21-24

As mentioned, the Indians include those whom the Book of Mormon call *Lamanites*. By the time of Christ's visit many had united with the Nephites and they participated in His visit too. (They renewed their hostilities later.) So their Indian descendants could have traditions of this event through the generations and adapt it in their cultural lore.

Specifically, Christ came to the city of Bountiful where the temple was located, where there had been a "great and marvelous change" in the land caused by the cataclysm. (3 Nephi 11:1-10) This change would be the widening of the narrow neck of land told of earlier, since it was in the land Bountiful. (p. 12, 13) The narrow pass survived for it is mentioned afterward. Mormon 3:5

Christ and Quetzalcoatl: Indian tradition in Latin America tells of a deity linked with a natural disaster who came to their ancestors. This was unknown when the Book of Mormon was first published. He is described as a "white bearded god." In various Indian cultures he had other names but *Quetzalcoatl,* the Aztec name, is generally used.

He fits the visit of Christ told in the Book of Mormon. The visit, natural disaster, and conduct of *Quetzalcoatl,* are hallmarks that intimate a cultural memory of the resurrected Christ visiting their forefathers.

For example, as cited, traditions of "the benevolent deity" *Quetzalcoatl* are linked to a great natural disaster as Christ is in the Book of Mormon. ("benevolent:" Prescott, p. 38,39,171) In the national palace in Mexico City there is a mural depicting the cataclysm and visit. (Fig. 5, next page) The photograph available was rather dark but a drawing below identifies the main elements. Some interpretations take it as myth. The one cited below fits Indian lore.

Fig. 5: Mural (about 1929) by Diego Rivera, noted Mexican artist.

Quetzalcoatl is shown in the air in his "serpent skiff," descending from heaven. And he is shown with a few men seated before him as if teaching them. (The Book of Mormon tells of Christ teaching a small group of special disciples so they could teach the people. 3 Nephi 11:21-41;12:1) The dark band at the top is darkness from volcanic cloud caused in a great cataclysm, and the sun upside down represents it not being seen in daytime due to that darkness. (Grant G. Pitcher citing palace guide - pers. comm.) The volcano has the Quetzalcoatl feathered serpent motif in its flames, linking this event to him.

The Book of Mormon says there was a "vapor of darkness" with three days of darkness, in which no "candles, neither torches;

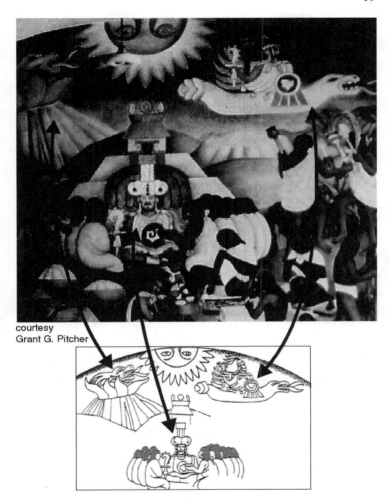

courtesy
Grant G. Pitcher

Figure 5 mural, National Palace, Mexico City

neither...fire" could be lighted. (3 Nephi 8:20-23) The vapor of darkness that prevented the lighting of candles, torches and fires indicate the presence of volcanic cloud of gas and dust. So these effects match. And Quetzalcoatl is shown fair-skinned, as with portrayals of Christ.

An Indian account tells of the event, saying "the earth shook, and the rocks were rent asunder." And it says this was on "the same date when Christ our Lord suffered." Toltec tradition (quoting Ixtlilxochitl; this booklet p.14) cited in *The Works of H.H. Bancroft*, v.5, p.210

CORRELATION: Quetzalcoatl being Christ is endorsed by the geologic findings – for the geologic event told in the Book of Mormon came about because of Christ's death and before His visit, and in Indian lore Quetzalcoatl is also connected with a cataclysm as noted above. The Book of Mormon says the earthquake part of the event "did shake the earth as if it was about to divide asunder." (3 Nephi 8:6) Then the resurrected Christ "descended out of heaven" to teach His *sheep* in this other fold as the Bible says he would. (3 Ne. 11:8; 15:21) And Quetzalcoatl, as noted, taught the Indians' ancestors.

The name *Quetzalcoatl* is composed of the Aztec terms *quetzal* for the beautiful Quetzal bird of Central America and *coatl* meaning *serpent.* Quetzalcoatl was called "god of the air." W. H. Prescott, *History of the Conquest of Mexico*, p.171
"*Quetzalcoatl* signifies 'feathered serpent.'" Prescott, p.39

"Moses made a serpent of brass" which the Lord told him to lift it up on a pole. This was done when the Israelites in the wilderness were bitten by snakes. Whoever looked upon the brass serpent would live. (Numbers 21:8,9) Christ shows the brass serpent to be symbolic of Him when He said, "As Moses lifted up the serpent...even so must the Son of Man be lifted up: that whosoever believeth in him should not perish...." John 3:14,15

Some think that saying "as" the serpent was lifted does not mean Christ related Himself to a serpent. But a meaning of *as* states, "in the aspect...of." (Webster) This is the very thing in Christ's statement. So this opposite view tries to deny a link between Christ and the serpent symbolism in *Quetzalcoatl*.

In spite of objections, many things connected with *Quetzalcoatl* indicate this name was used for an Indian recollection of Christ visiting the Americas in ancient times – such as Quetzalcoatl ushering in a period of peace. And this is what Christ did when He came; initiated a long period of peace. 4 Nephi 1:13

Periods of time agree: The Book of Mormon says this period of peace began to fade 200 years after His birth and decayed further to another stage 305 years after his birth. (4 Ne. 1:1, 2, 13, 24, 45-47) Indian tradition says the people "lived in peace for two hundred years" after the coming of Quetzalcoatl, who came following the great natural cataclysm when "the earth shook."

> period of peace: Grant G. Pitcher (friend) quoting guide at the mural of Quetzalcoatl in National Palace, Mexico City, pers. comm.

An Indian history from Mexico says "It was 305 years" after the cataclysm that certain people "began to usurp the kingdom...after... many years of peace."

> Mexican historian, Ixtlilxochitl, circa 1600, Spanish to English, 1939 by Arnulfo Rodriguez, Univ. of California

It is notable that Indian histories speak of 200 and 305 year marks in relation to the loss of peace in the land, as does the Book of Mormon. (Indian history dates these periods from the calamity rather than Christ's birth but still, the 200 and 305 year periods match the Book of Mormon stating these lengths of time.)

Quetzalcoatl assessed: Scholars assume Quetzalcoatl was an extra-ordinary Indian whom later generations venerated. But he is described as being "tall in stature, with a white skin...and flowing beard, so unlike the Indian physiogomy." (Prescott, p.171) So the idea that Quetzalcoatl was an Indian is not tenable, especially when the Mexican artist who painted the mural in Fig. 5 in accordance with Indian tradition shows him fair-skinned. Quetzalcoatl's fair skin is all the more evident with the Indian figures being dark-skinned.

The mural artist painted Quetzalcoatl so he looks like typical portrayals of Jesus Christ. Did he know something that indicated Quetzalcoatl was Christ or was this his own perception consciously or subconsciously? The similarity seems rather strong to be by chance. But regardless of this and the likeness, he held to the general Indian tradition that Quetzalcoatl was fair-skinned.

Among the Indians who honored *Quetzalcoatl* by this and other names, the Aztecs in particular perverted their worship of the "benevolent" Quetzalcoatl by turning to human sacrifice. But in their culture, sacrifice was not limited to the worship of Quetzalcoatl for all the "altars....of the numerous Aztec gods, were stained with human blood." (Prescott, p. 263, 4) So there is no need to doubt similarities between Christ and Quetzalcoatl as "benevolent." ˙

Critics of the Book of Mormon dismiss the idea of Quetzalcoatl being Christ, citing the name being used by very unChrist-like individuals. But this does not do away with the original personage.

And critics tell of him being represented as black at times, but we have the *Black Madonna* in Poland representing Mary although she was obviously not black. Likewise, black portrayals of Quetzalcoatl do not dismiss the fair-skinned tradition. Some say the name *Quetzalcoatl* came long after Book of Mormon times. But so what? This name and others used by various Indian peoples represent an evolving cultural lore of an original personage from earlier times.

At least one critic says LDS scholars discount Quetzalcoatl being Christ. (Johnson, *Quetzalcoatl: Jesus in the Americas?* paper) Actually, it is just that LDS scholars advise caution in attributing correlations to Christ since some Indian leaders took the name later on and this can confuse the issue.   e.g. John L. Sorenson, *An American Setting for the Book of Mormon*, p. 326-30

Summary: Findings of a great geologic upheaval fit the Book of Mormon account. Christ speaks of going to *other sheep* and Indian accounts tell of the deity Quetzalcoatl who visited their ancestors. Both the Book of Mormon and Indian sources tell of peace ushered in by a geologic calamity when the respective visits were made and each cite 200 and 305 year marks in that peace coming to an end.

There is no way Joseph Smith or anyone else in his day could know of this geologic upheaval "about the time of Christ," of Quetzalcoatl as the basis to fabricate Christ in ancient America, and of these specific time-spans in previously unknown Indian history, to fraudulently include in a book in 1830. These things did not even come to light until long after the death of Joseph Smith.

Quetzalcoatl adds to the geologic evidence since he is linked to a great geologic calamity as shown by the erupting volcano in the mural and Indian lore, as Christ is linked to the geologic event told of in the Book of Mormon.

GEOGRAPHY: By showing that the geologic findings fit the geography evident in the Book of Mormon account, we can know that the geologic findings are not unrelated changes that just seem to fit the Book of Mormon. This involves detail that requires some close attention but helps to show the consistency between the Book of Mormon and the real world.

The lands north and south of the Motagua Fault Zone fit the lands

24

that were north and south of the neck of land, for the fit between the text, the Zone, and adjacent geography is exact in every detail. This shows the uplift in the Zone indeed fits the Book of Mormon event.

RIVER SIDON: (Fig. 6) The Sidon, the only river identified in the Book of Mormon, was in the land southward which was bounded by seas *east* and *west*. (Appendix, p. 49) Its headwaters were to the south. Alma 22:27

It flowed north. (Except for winding in various directions as with any river.) Its mouth was near the neck of land. (see Fig. 6)

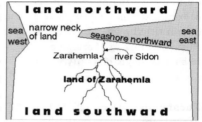

Figure 6 Sidon and Zarahemla

Details: There is mention of east and west of the Sidon but none to north and south of it to show it turned east or west to empty into the sea. (It is typically thought that the neck of land was an 'hourglass' shape and the Sidon turned to the sea east or west.) So where did it reach the sea?

To the north the east sea extended west to the neck of land. (see Fig. 6) With the east sea extending west, the land southward would have a north seacoast and the Book of Mormon shows it had a "seashore northward" where it could empty into the sea. (see Fig. 6) (Appendix, p. 47) It was a short river. Appendix, p. 51-53

CORRELATION: (Fig. 7) The Ulúa river in northwest Honduras is only 125 miles long. It flows north as did the Sidon, and empties into the Gulf of Honduras which is an extension of the Caribbean Sea, which fits as the sea east. The Gulf of Honduras provides a seashore northward where the Ulúa empties into the sea as the river Sidon would.

The Ulúa, being southward and rather near the Motagua Fault Zone, fits the Sidon's proximity to the narrow neck of land. (Although locally it is east. [See Fig. 7] But the full landmass of course extends further south to Panama.)

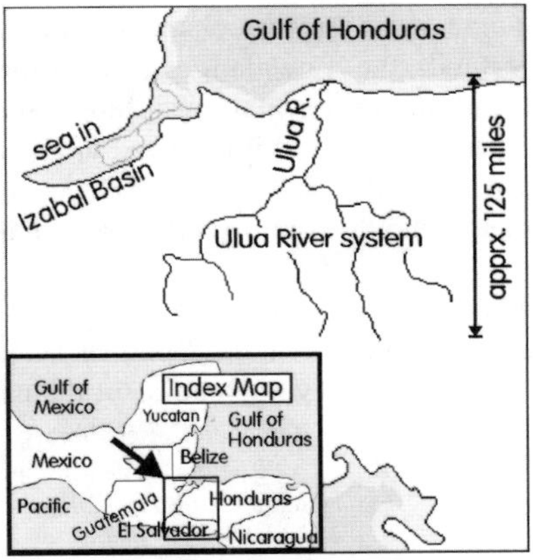

Figure 7 Ulúa River

Zarahemla: The Nephites' capital city of Zarahemla was on the west bank of the river Sidon. Alma 6:7

CORRELATION: The name *Zurahuma* can be reconstituted on the west bank of the Ulúa. This name, obviously very much like *Zarahemla*, is found in a context and setting that fits the Book of Mormon *Zarahemla* in every way.

Details: The city of Zarahemla was founded and named by another people who came from Jerusalem and integrated with the Nephites. They of course spoke Hebrew to begin with. (Omni vs. 12-15; Mormon 9:33) The name *Zarahemla* fits as a composite of the Hebrew words: *zara*, to sow, and *hemla*, a blend of words that amount to *full*. (*hem*, abundance and *mala*, overflowing; *Strong's Concordance*) In the early Spanish period the Ulúa flood plain, now called the *Sula* plain or valley, was the *Valle de Zura*.

Doris Stone, *Archaeology of the North Coast of Honduras*, Memoirs of the Peabody Museum, Harvard., v. IX, #1, 1941; appdx. *Relaciones de Yucatan*

Z and *s* can be interchanged. For example *Zion* can be *Sion*. In Nahuatl, the Aztec language used for a time in the Zura/Sula valley, the phoneme or sound *r* was "lost" and replaced by *l*. (Denison, *Primitive Aryans of America*) It influenced the local tongue. Thus, *Sula* and *Zura* are "synonymous." (Stone) *Zura* is nearly identical to *Zara* in *Zarahemla* and their context shows them to be the same place, as follows.

There was a "chief" Indian town of *Sula (Zura)* that faded to insignificance when the Spanish set their headquarters west of the Zura/Sula valley at Naco. But the names *Zura* and *Sula* endured.

Hernando Cortés; library of CIRMA (Centro de Investigaciones Regionales de Mesoamérica) Antigua, Guatemala; Robert S. Chamberlain, *The Conquest and Colonization of Honduras 1502-1550, Carnegie Institution of Washington, publication 598, 1953*

Knowledge of Sula/Zura's location was lost. (Chamberlain) The Spanish had built a town near Sula/Zura. Therefore this Spanish town would be a marker for the area where Sula/Zura was located.

The village of *La Buena Esperanza* is about three miles west of the Ulúa. (Honduran govt. map) Its name has elements of the Spanish town's name; *Santa Maria de la Buena Esperanza*. Nearby is the surface site Santana with archaeological pits, which fits as Sula/Zura. (Fig. 8)

The name *La Buena Esperanza* does not mean this present-day village is necessarily on the site of the original Spanish town, but the distance from Naco's site to this village fits with the recorded distance from Naco to the Spanish town. So it is evident that Sula/Zura was near the site of the present village which fits with Santana as outlined below.

The lack of ruins may seem inconsistent for an important site. But Zarahemla was built of wood as shown by it evidently burning completely since it had to be rebuilt after the earthquake and volcanic

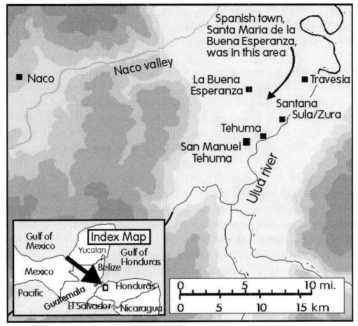

Figure 8 Sula/Zura valley

destruction at the time of Christ's death. (3 Nephi 8:8; 4 Nephi 1:8) For Zarahemla to be built of wood, the Sidon valley would have been forested to provide the wood. The Ulúa valley fits for it was forested until cleared for large commercial farms (fincas) beginning in the late 1800s.   George Byron Gordon, *Researches in the Oloa* (sic) *Valley,*
Memoirs of the Peabody Museum of American Archaeology
and Ethnology, Harvard, v. 1, #4, 1898

The Indians abandoned the ancient cities of Mesoamerica. The cities of stone and cement became overgrown by jungle growth and disintegration set it. And even more so, a neglected city of wood, as Zarahemla would be, would decay in the humid forest environment. (Zarahemla was fought over and finally abandoned to the Lamanites who would have no attachment to repair and maintain it.)

Mormon 2:27-29

But place-names can linger at or near a site as shown below. The evident site of the former chief Indian town of *Zura/Sula* continued to be used as *Santa Ana* or *Santana* until it was finally cleared not long after 1928. (Many Indian sites received Spanish names. So *Santana-/Santa Ana* for *Zura/Sula* is consistent.) Another name nearby also indicates Santana is the site of Sula/Zura. (See next page.)

Only wood is mentioned for buildings in the land southward. (e.g. Jarom vs. 8) Since the Ulúa valley (in the evident land southward) lacks suitable stone, wood and adobe was used. (Gordon) This fits with the setting for the city of Zarahemla with its wood construction. But in the Maya era, after Book of Mormon times, suitable stone was imported to Travesia about four miles north of Santana and small pyramids built. (see Fig. 8) (Stone) These have also been cleared for commercial farms.   George Hasemann, Instituto Hondureño de Antrolopogia e Historia, Tegucigalpa, Honduras, pers. comm.

Travesia was the ceremonial center. Sula/Zura was at the center of several villages that existed when the Spanish came. (*Relaciones*) Since they were close together, this suggests they shared the same population base.

Babylon – a place-name precedent: *Babylon* is Greek for that city's name which was *Babu-ella*. Its chief temple was *é-sag-illa*. (New Catholic Encyclopedia, vol. II, p. 3,4) Within ten miles of the ruins of *Babylon/Babu-ella* are the cities of *Babil* and *Hillah*. (Hammond Atlas) The first *H* in *Hillah* is an Arab pre-fix so this name would originally be *Illah*. (*illah*)   Dilworth Parkinson, linguist in Arabic, personal comm.

These names are of course similar to components of *Babu-ellu* and *é-sag-illa*. And these forms of these components are retained near their point of origin.

Significance of names in the Sula/Zura valley: About two miles south of Santana was the village of Tehuma. (see Fig. 8) It was swept away by flood in 1936. Its name is significant along with *Zura,* as shown below. The now-vanished village of Tehuma is prominent on a "historical and archaeological map" made before 1936, showing its local importance. Borbolla, Daniel. F. Rubin and Rivas, Pedro, *Honduras: Monu mentos Historicos y Arqueologicos* U.N.S.C.O. y Consejo Internacional de la Filosofia y de Las Ciencias Humanas, Mexico D.F., 1953

The name *Tehuma* is preserved in the name of the municipal seat, *San Manuel Tehuma*, three miles southwest of Santana. (see Fig. 8) The name *Tehuma* included in the name of the municipal seat indicates this is the area's name.

Te- in *Tehuma* is an Aztec pre-fix. Before the coming of the Spanish the Aztecs had considerable influence in the Sula/Zura valley and the local Indians also used this prefix, probable due to Aztec influence. Edward Conzemius, *International Journal of American Linguistics*, nos. 3-4, p.169

Without the pre-fix *Te-*, the name would of course be *Huma. (huma)* So we find the names *Zura* and *Huma* within three miles or so of each other. With *babu-ella/illa* as a precedent, we see that *Zura* and *huma* could combine as *Zurahuma* which is much like *Zarahemla.*

This similarity is significant when we realize vowels are "unstable" and are frequently substituted over a period of time. (Denison, see Appendix p. 43) For example, *London* was *Londinium* when founded by the Romans. The *-ium* was a Latin suffix, leaving the Roman/Latin original as *Londin* compared with *London* now. With *Zara* to *Zura* we have a similar situation.

Zura and *huma* for *Zurahuma* are just west of the Ulúa and fit the geologic/geographic setting of *Zarahemla* beside the Sidon. There is more that indicates the more similar name *Zurahumla* but is too involved for this overview.

Location? But just where was Zarahemla located? Likely it was not Travesia even though it had pyramids, for it developed after Book of Mormon times. And probably it was not Tehuma since there is no trace of it as likely of a city even after a flood.

Santana is the likely place since this is only site on the west bank still evident out of all the sites obliterated by clearing for large farms.

Since it can still be identified, this suggests that like the tip of an iceberg, this site marks the location of a substantial city as Zarahemla would have been. But whether the site is Santana or some other known or undiscovered site, we have neighboring names that can combine as *Zurahuma* or even *Zurahumla*.

Summary: *Zura* and *huma* are in a well-defined area, the Ulúa/Sula-/Zura valley. This valley fits as the original land of Zarahemla which became the *land of Zarahemla* in a state sense when the Nephites expanded their territory and also called it the *land of Zarahemla*.

The names that fit *Zarahemla* are southward of the Motagua Fault Zone as Zarahemla was in the land southward of the neck of land. These names, and the Ulúa as the Sidon, enhance the significance of the nearby geologic findings in the Motagua Fault Zone that indicate the location of the narrow neck of land.

Therefore, this nearby geography supports the geologic changes in the Motagua Fault Zone being evidence of the land widening here in the great geologic event told in the Book of Mormon.

GEOGRAPHIC MARKER IN LAND NORTHWARD: The geology in the Motagua Fault Zone that shows the neck of land was here is also enhanced by the identification of a peninsula just north of it, in the land northward.

Details: *Desolation* was the southernmost land in the land northward. (Fig. 9) It bordered on Bountiful where the narrow neck of land was located.

Alma 22:32; Ether 7:6 Nephites colonized in the north, but only in the land Desolation, "from the sea south to the sea north, from the sea west to the sea east."

Helaman 3:6,8

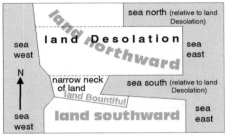

Figure 9 peninsula in land Desolation

Only seas east and west are told of up to now. This verse interjects seas north and south that help identify the geographic marker referred to. That is, the only way for the land Desolation to be surrounded by four seas would be for it to include a peninsula. (see Fig. 9)

If the neck of land was gradual as typically visualized, there could be no seas north and south of the land Desolation, for the east and west coasts of the neck of land would meld with the coasts of Desolation and the rest of the land northward. There would just be more sea east and west. Only the inclusion of a peninsula fits the description.

CORRELATION: The Yucatan Peninsula, immediately north of the Motagua Fault Zone, has this configuration that fits in every way. (Fig. 10, next page) And it has ruins located where they fit the Book of Mormon account. Appendix, p. 53

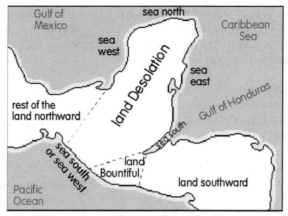

Figure 10 land Desolation

Details: Fig. 10 (This of course varies from Figure 9 which is only a diagrammatic representation of what the text says.) With the sea in the Izabal Basin cutting in below the Yucatan Peninsula there would be a sea to the *south*. The Gulf of Mexico would be the *sea west* and the Pacific would be another element of the *sea south* or the *sea west*. The sea*s north* and *east* are obvious.

Some say the seas north and south are regional references to the seas east and west. But it speaks of events "on the west sea, south." (Alma 53:8) So it is evident that the east and west seas kept their directional names regardless of region as indicated by this description involving a region to the south beside the west sea. Others consider the seas *north* and *south* to be "metaphorical" but admit they consider it only a possibility. The Yucatan Peninsula provides an actual place that fits the description in the Book of Mormon that mentions four seas.

CONCLUSION: Earlier we saw that the geology of Lake Ilopango marks the land southward. And we have seen how the Uluá river and the names beside it regarding Zarahemla also indicate the land southward. Now we see that the Yucatan Peninsula fits as the peninsula just north of the narrow neck of land.

These geographic features, next to the Motagua Fault Zone, reinforce the geologic signs that the neck of land was indeed here. And as seen earlier, the Motagua Valley and Guatemala Depression, matching as the narrow pass, also show the neck of land was in the Zone.

All of these findings taken together fit as the evidence of the geologic event foretold, in the right geographic setting. And since the Book of Mormon tells of the event, and foretold the findings in 1830 long before the event was ever known, they testify of its authenticity.

As observed earlier, a secondary benefit is how the findings show where Book of Mormon lands were located and therefore provide the means to better understand its events.

The findings also account for two other geographic features told of in the Book of Mormon that have a bearing on the events it tells about – a narrow strip of wilderness that separated the Nephites and Lamanites, and the hill Cumorah where the Nephite nation was destroyed. But they are less directly connected to the geologic evidence since they are farther from the Motagua Fault Zone so they are briefly outlined in the appendix. Appendix, p. 57, 60

Still, the major purpose in these findings is their testimony of Jesus Christ and temporal testimony that the Book of Mormon is true.

There are those who want to impose their own test upon the Book of Mormon, but this would be like a judge throwing out a litigant's prepared evidence and telling him what evidence he must use.

And evidence can exist which is not yet be known.

For example, the Bible mentions copper but scholars doubted the Bible in this matter since no evidence of copper had been found. (Ezra 8:27) Then signs of ancient copper smelters were found south of the Dead Sea. It is likewise with the Book of Mormon. Critics doubt certain physical things it tells about for which no ample evidence has yet been found. So they take this as an issue to try to discredit the Book of Mormon.

However, more evidence is coming to light. For example, the Book of Mormon tells of horses while it is said they were extinct in Book of Mormon times. But evidence for horses in this period has been found. (Appendix, p. 71-77) And critics overlook the Bible mentioning things which took considerable time to verify.

For instance, the Bible tells of Ezion-Geber, a large industrial port on Gulf of Aqaba on the Red Sea, but its location was unknown. So its existence was questioned until discovered in 1936, mostly covered by sand. Most of Mesoamerica has dense forest cover so it is even more difficult to find artifacts and even structures. And study here is relatively recent compared with Bible lands.

So if archaeologists don't stumble onto things that critics want, it does not mean the Book of Mormon is false! Rather, the Book of Mormon tells of evidence that has been found and can be objectively examined.

So instead of insisting on unfound evidence to just find fault, one should examine evidence that has been found. Still, over time, evidence that is wanted can come to light as with the Bible. In the meantime we have various types of evidence. In particular, we have this literally rock-solid evidence that was foretold and has been found.

What Now?

To accept a thing as true, a person wants evidence that it is true. In a court of law the criteria is whether a thing is "true beyond reasonable doubt." But in spite of clear evidence, some will object to a thing on unreasonable grounds. Some can be so insistent on their preconceptions they will dismiss any other view without examining it. Or one will not give real thought to a new thing or will accept someone else's negative view.

Yet some welcome new ideas to broaden their view and want the truth on significant issues.

This is only a sketch of the findings. But still, it shows beyond reasonable doubt on a material level that the Book of Mormon is true, for as noted earlier, there is no way the things foretold and found could be known in 1830. In addition, there is a spiritual way to determine its truthfulness as noted earlier. It is often called *Moroni's Promise*.

This was made by the last Nephite prophet, Moroni, who journeyed from Mesoamerica to bury the Book of Mormon plates where they could be revealed years later to fulfill the Lord's purposes. He said,

> And when ye shall receive these things, I would exhort you that ye would ask God, the Eternal Father, in the name of Christ, if these things are not true; and if ye shall ask with a sincere heart, with real intent, having faith in Christ, he will manifest the truth of it unto you, by the power of the Holy Ghost. Moroni 10:4

So it is a matter of praying about "these things;" the Book of Mormon. This is treated as if reading the Book of Mormon with sincerity and intent and asking if it is true is enough. But notice the inclusion of *not* in the promise. This usually negative word has great implications in this kind of context as the Bible shows in the following.

Two disciples met the Savior after His resurrection but did not recognize Him at first. Later they recounted finally recognizing Him, for "they said one to another, Did **not** our heart burn within us, while he talked with us by the way, and while he opened to us the scriptures?"

Luke 24:32 emphasis added

They did not ask "did our heart burn?" The inclusion of *not* means each had this feeling within his bosom and confirmed it to each other.

Another example is a lawyer asking a question in court. He (or she) should not ask unless he already knows the answer or has good reason to believe he knows and wants confirmation. *Not* is included in such as asking a witness, "Is it not true that you" did such and such?

We use this form of question in everyday life, but in a contracted form. For instance, a mother might say to her child, "Didn't I tell you to look both ways before you cross the street?" The mother knows she did and believes the child remembers. Or one might say to a friend at the end of a day, "Isn't that a beautiful sunset?" The one who asks expects there will be agreement. For us, using *not* without contraction seems formal for everyday talk, but either way, *not* is used to confirm what is already believed or known.

The inclusion of *not* in the promise means one has to believe the Book of Mormon is true or could be, and then ask for confirmation of this conclusion. This is implied by Moroni saying "receive these things" before asking. Receive includes "accept." Reading it, reflection, study of evidence, praying during the process, and allowing oneself to be touched by its spirit, are factors to help accept it.

Many have learned it is true without realizing the implications of *not* in the promise for they already gained the belief it requires before asking. (This was my experience) This belief leads many to gradually obtain a confirmation without explicitly asking. But there are those who don't get confirmation for they only ask, for just asking, even with sincerity and intent, does not fully meet Moroni's requirements.

Those who accept the Book of Mormon are influenced by things such as the example of Latter-day Saints they know and/or study with LDS missionaries. This booklet shows you there is valid evidence. Latter-day Saints believe the Bible as do other Christians. The Book of Mormon is probably the greatest visible difference.

Finding the truth: Many turn down an invitation to learn about these things for they are "too busy," have encountered negative ideas about the 'Mormon' Church, and/or feel what they have is enough, whether spiritual or material. Yet many recognize there is a spiritual aspect to consider or reconsider, and many religions claim the way.

Now we have a young man, Joseph Smith, who prayed to know which church was true and was told none was because Christianity had strayed from its original principles. But it would be restored through him. He claimed revelations and authority from heaven to restore the gospel and Church of Christ as it was originally.

He said the Book of Mormon is the "keystone" of it all and the evidence foretold supports this keystone. And Moroni made a promise.

What conclusion? As stated, the purpose of this booklet is to show predicted evidence of the divinity of Jesus Christ and the authenticity of the Book of Mormon. This is a great test the Book of Mormon gives itself – that certain evidence would be found – for if this evidence did not exist, it would discredit itself.

If Joseph Smith made this all up, he inadvertently included something that would show the Book of Mormon is a fraud. For if the evidence did not exist, this would discredit him and the book and the church he says he founded under divine direction.

One might argue it is coincidence that a geologic event as told in the Book of Mormon did take place. But one cannot reasonably argue that the high degree of agreement between the Book of Mormon event and the one identified by geologists and archaeologists are coincidence! Agreement is too extensive and detailed.

Since there is no way this geologic information could be known in 1830, a divine source is the only feasible answer. This offers "cause" to consider the truthfulness of the Book of Mormon.

New scripture? Most people in all religions doubt God would provide scripture in our day since the typical view says God did so anciently but not now. For instance, a statement in the Bible's Book of Revelation is taken to mean that revelation and scripture have ceased. It says, "If any man shall add unto these things, God shall add unto him the plagues that are written in this book." Revelation 22:18

But the Bible is a collection of "little books" written separately and compiled as the Bible. The book *Revelation* was written in the first century AD but was not the last book written just because it is last in the Bible. For example, scholars have generally concluded that John wrote his gospel after he wrote the book *Revelation*.

On this basis the warning for "man" to not "add unto these things" would apply only to the Book of Revelation. Even if it was the last book and did apply to the Bible, God could add whatever He wanted.

Besides, an earlier reference in the Bible, says "Ye shall not add unto the word which I command you." (Deuteronomy 4:2) Does this mean all

written after this statement in the Bible should not have been recorded? Obviously not. This simply shows that such prohibitions about
adding to scriptural writing is limited to the specific writing involved.
Therefore, the Book of Mormon containing revelation does not conflict with the Bible. Besides, it states support for the Bible, and the
Bible itself foretells the Book of Mormon. Appendix, p. 61-68

God gave guidance in the past as in the Bible but there have been
many interpretations of what it says. And there are many other faiths.
Whether a Christian sect or another religion, each is built on the word
of its founder. (Appendix, p. 78-81) But there is more than the word of
Joseph Smith – Book of Mormon evidence foretold and found.

To summarize: The Book of Mormon tells of an ancient people
whose rise and fall are instructive for us. For, as we have competing
voices that declare a particular theology or emphasize the pursuit of
worldly things and pleasures, people of the Book of Mormon had the
same choices to make. The people who were righteous at first even-
tually faltered and fell in battle about 400 AD. The victors were those
we call *Indians* and include people such as the *Maya* and *Aztecs*.

The appendix that follows provides additional insights and evidence.
A map that shows the overall setting for the findings then follows.

The Book of Mormon is clearly written. (Except for quotes from
Isaiah which you may want to skip for now.) As the findings show,
there is evidence to show it is true beyond reasonable doubt. Reading
it reveals its narrative, spirit, and value. And although it may be hard
for some to see, it promises a spiritual insight for those who seek it.

FULL RESEARCH: It needs to be emphasized that the material in
this presentation and the appendix comprise only an overview or outline. Therefore, questions may arise that are not answered here.

Appendix

PLACE-NAMES: One of the cities sunk and covered by a lake was built by the Lamanites. They had named it "Jerusalem, calling it after the land of their fathers' nativity." The area around it was the *land of Jerusalem*. (Alma 21:1,2) Correlations can be made with this name.

Several steps are needed for these correlations that may seem a little complex. But they are not all that difficult to follow.

In the Spanish colonization of Latin America "hybrid" place-names were sometimes formed by adding Spanish suffixes to Aztec words. But "occasionally...a Spanish word received an Aztecan suffix."

> Holmer, Nils M., *Indian Placenames in Mexico and CentralAmerica,* Essays and Studies on American Language and Literature, XVI, Upsala University, Copenhagen, 1964, p. 27

The town of *Nacendelan* is shown on early maps near Lake Ilopango in El Salvador. (e.g., Fig. 11, next page) This fits as a hybrid name with Indian and Spanish elements that refer to a place of birth as with the Lamanite Jerusalem. It includes the Spanish *de,* meaning *of* or *from* plus the Aztec place-name ending, *-lan*. It matches as:

> *Nacen-de-lan:* "they-are-born-of-place"
> Spanish   Aztec

Nacendelan: (Fig. 11) There are distortions in this map as on all early maps. (*Nicaragua* is too far north. The city of "*Guatimala*" [sic] is too close to the lake and to *Nicaragua*. The river is fanciful.)

The pronoun *they* and the verb *born,* for *Nacendelan*, may seem out of place in a place-name but the Aztecs used "sentence-words" which included verbs and they had a "pre-occupation with...person identification." Richard J. Andrews, *Introduction to Classical Nahuatl,* Un iversity of Texas Press, 1975, p. xii, xiii

Figure 11 Nacendelan on 1597 map (upper right)

Although the Aztecs named places for local features as common with
any people, they did not invariably do so. For example, Aztecs from
Mexico went with the Spanish in their conquests to the south in Central America and invented their own names for places taken. *Quet-*
zaltenango is an Aztec name given by them in the middle of the Ma-
yan culture of Guatemala. It means "the place of the Quetzal (bird)."
Alcaldé's office, Quetzaltenango; correspondence

And *Huehuetenango*, also in the midst of the Maya of Guatemala,
was coined by the Aztecs from Mexico and means "place of the
ancients." (Municipalidad Huehuetenago; correspondence) *Huehuetenango* for
"place of the ancients" is obviously "person identification."

As for *Nacendelan* at Lake Ilopango, the inclusion of *they* fits a name
invented by the Aztecs related to "person" to describe the actual
place-name used by the Indians at Lake Ilopango.

Specifically, this fits as reference to "person identification" and birth,
which fits the Lamanite Jerusalem named for the original Jerusalem

in honor of where their ancestors were born. Also, the actual name of
this town at Lake Ilopango also relates to the name *Jerusalem*.

Cojutepque: The city of *Cojutepeque* is in the same position relative
to Lake Ilopango as *Nacendelan,* indicating two names for the same
place. (*Nacendelan* being the Aztec name describing the local Indian
name.) A census of Indian towns in 1548 reveals that *Cojutepeque*
was spelled *Cuxutepeque* by the Spanish and pronounced *Cushutepec*. (David Browning, *El Salvador Landscape and Society*, p. 305) This pro-
nunciation pattern is reinforced by the nearby Indian town spelled
and pronounced *Teshutepec*.

The Book of Mormon was written with "the learning of the Jews" in
"reformed Egypian." (1 Ne. 1:2; Mormon 9:32) Elements like those in the
Egyptian and Jewish names for *Jerusalem* are in the Indian pronun-
ciation *Cushutepec*, indicating the name survived in the vicinity of
the original Lamanite city. (Alma 21:1,2) (As elements of the name for
Babylon survived in Iraq. p. 28)

First, *Cushutepec* breaks down as *C-ushu-tepec*.

     C- and *-tepec* are place-name elements. (Like the prefix *new*
and suffix *ton* are sometimes used for place-names in English.)

              Nils M. Holmer, p.14; Diccionario Geografico. v. 3, p. 264

Second, by deleting the elements *C* and *tepec,* we find the root for
Cushutepec is *ushu* which we will see indicates a link with the name
Jerusalem which was formed from two root words anciently:

     – Hebrew*: Yeru-shalayim, Yeru-shalim, etc.*

     – Egyptian: *'ru-shalimum*

     – Assyrian and Babylonian: *Uru-shalimmu*

                  various biblical encyclopedias

The resulting *u-sha or usha,* created by combining these root words,
is only one letter different than the root *ushu* in *Cushutepec*. But
usha is not the root for *Yerushalayim*, etc. It just happens to result

where its two root words join. (e.g. *Yeru-shalayim*) And it is the same with this Egyptian name. Yet over time these adjoining roots could be taken to be the root. But whether so or not, there is an Egyptian name for *Jerusalem* with a root that stands alone.

That is, another Egyptian name for Jerusalem was *Aushamen*. (*Sacramentum Verbi*, v. 2, p. 409) The *mn* or *men* element is an Egyptian suffix that means "without end." So the root, *ausha*, stands alone. (Dr. Alan Fletcher, Egyptologist, pers. comm.) So let us consider this root *ausha* since the Book of Mormon was written in "reformed Egyptian," to see if *ausha* could actually be the basis for the root *ushu* in *Cushutepec*. (The Book of Mormon being written in *its* form of "reformed Egyptian fits Egyptian being simplified or modified or *reformed* anciently, from *Hieroglyphics* to *Hieretic* to *Demotic*.)

What follows may seem technical, but is enlightening. It takes historical language development into account. This would apply to *reformed Egyptian* as with other languages.

1. "Vowels are unstable" and *a* may become *au*.
                    T.S. Denison, *The Primitive Aryans of America,* 1908, p. 93
Ausha in the Egyptian name for Jerusalem could become *aushau*. The likelihood of adding *u* to the final *a* to produce *aushau* is evident with the prevalence of *u* in the ancient forms for *Jerusalem* noted.

2. "In the historical development of languages...*au* (becomes) *u'* or *o.*"   M. Langdon, *Comparative Hokan-Coahuitlan Studies*, p.43
Since *u* prevails in these ancient forms, it is evident that both instances of *au* in the above root (*aushau*) would become *u* and not *o,* resulting in *ushu*.

To summarize: Starting with the free-standing Egyptian root *ausha* – we would end up with *ushu*. That is, *ausha* to *aushau* to *ushu*.

Since *ushu* is the root of the original name for Cojutepeque beside Lake Ilopango – pronounced *Cushutepec* – a link is evident since it is found in the right geologic setting for the site of the buried and lake-covered Lamanite city of Jerusalem.

Another view: Regarding the name *Nacendelan*, an authority on Central American history says hybrid names came late in the Spanish colonial period. (James Lockhart, UCLA prof. of Central American history, pers. comm.)But regardless of written records, "old maps... often indicate... (things about) which the written documents are silent."

Proceedings of the American Antiquarian Society,
re: Spanish cartography, 1909, p.369

Maps place *Nacendelan* early in the Spanish period. (e.g. moderately early map, p. 41) The authority cited assumes *Nacendelan* is from an Aztec name. He concludes it is from *nanche*, a fruit. (Lockhart,pers. Comm.) But only the first two letters of *nacen* and *nanche* are alike and the other letters are in different order. And *ch* in *nanche* is not like *c* in *nacen*. He says *nanche* is likely from *nantzin* or "mother tree." He suggests *Nacendelan* is a Spanish form of an Aztec name, which he thinks could be something such as *Nantzintitlan*. It would mean "the place of the mother tree." But this name could suggest birth anyway since a mother gives birth. So his view could also fit.

Place-names: There are other names at Lake Ilopango that also relate to *Jerusalem* that fit and enhance the geologic evidence. They are in the full research.

NARROW NECK OF LAND OFFSET WEST: (Fig. 12) The neck of land was in the land Bountiful. This is seen by defenses set up there. (p. 70) The land of Bountiful was north of the west wilderness but separated by a narrow srip of wilderness that ran "round about" from sea to sea. (Alma 22:29-32) (p. 58) Since Bountiful was just north of the west wilderness, it was offset to the west. (Alma 22:29) And since the neck of land was in the land Bountiful it was also offset west.

NARROW NECK OF LAND ELIMINATED: Before the geologic event the neck of land is told of in the present tense, as "the place where the sea divides the land." (Ether 10:20) A gradual (hourglass) shape as commonly visualized (or any shape) would separate the seas. But how would the sea divide the land? The dividing of the land could not be total for that would mean two continents. In context of a neck of land, the sea would have to cut sharply into the land to "divide" it. (see Fig. 12) A gradual shape would not.

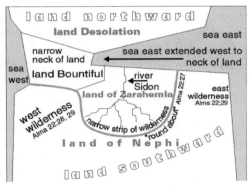

Figure 12 neck of land offset west

After the geologic event the lands in the land southward "**were** nearly surrounded by water." (Alma 22:32) Note how this description is in the past tense. (The first description, in the present tense, is quoted from a record made before the event. The second was written afterward.)

Figure 13 – Zone now up: It does not speak of the neck of land directly, but saying the lands in the land southward *were* nearly surrounded by water shows it was no longer. The past tense used here shows the neck of land had ceased to exist since being nearly surrounded was due to **"there being** a small neck of land." Alma 22:32

The loss of the neck of land and the land southward being no longer nearly surrounded, could happen only if the land widened in the event told of in the Book of Mormon. This fits the Motagua Fault Zone rising in the geologic event "about the time of Christ" identified by scientists, spilling the sea from the Izabal Basin and widening out the land. (see Fig. 3, p. 13)

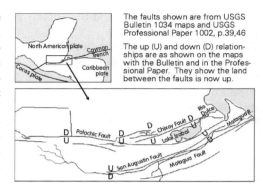

The faults shown are from USGS Bulletin 1034 maps and USGS Professional Paper 1002, p.39,46

The up (U) and down (D) relationships are as shown on the maps with the Bulletin and in the Professional Paper. They show the land between the faults is now up.

Figure 13 Major Faults in Motagua Fault Zone

Also, a fault opened that helped empty the basin by draining the sea out. A very short river, the Rio Dulce, now runs in this fault, draining water from Lake Izabal to the Gulf of Honduras. (Fig. 14) This fault is one of several that shows the Zone was elevated. (see Fig. 13) As noted earlier (p. 12, 13) research in the Izabal Basin shows this happened in the first century AD which fits the Book of Mormon geologic event at the time of Christ's death.

This change in the land is also indicated by the Nephites' change in their defense of the land northward. That is, they ceased to defend at the neck of land in the land Bountiful

Figure 14 Rio Dulce in course formed by fault

which gave them the most secure line of defense for it was the shortest distance from sea to sea. This indicates the location of the neck of land was no longer defensible. They later defended at the city Desolation in the land northward which ultimately failed.

Alma 52:9; Heleman 4:6,7; Mormon 3:5-7; 4:1,2

SEASHORE NORTHWARD: Nephite soldiers went to the seashore near the city of Mulek as decoys to draw out the Lamanites who had taken this city. It was "on the east borders by the seashore." (Alma 51: 26) It was within a day's march of the city Bountiful at the southern end of the narrow pass in the neck of land. (Fig. 4, p.14)

Alma 52:9

This short distance is seen in the military action described here, which all took place in one day, in which the Lamanites were lured to the city of Bountiful and defeated. (Alma 52:16-40) Specifically, we need to note that the Nephite decoys "began to retreat down by the seashore, northward." (Alma 52:23) Notice the comma. With the comma it has been thought that they fled north along the (east) coast that presumably lay in a north-south direction.

But texts with Middle East cultural roots, as the Book of Mormon is, are not punctuated or very little. So the typesetter for the first edition did most of it. (*Church History in the Fulness of Times*, p.65) He overdid the commas and editing since then has removed many, but not this one.

Without the comma it would of course read: "by the seashore northward." This would be a geographic descriptive form in Book of Mormon terminology as with the *land northward* and the *land southward*. A seashore or coast is a geographic factor too, so being named to fit a specific direction is consistent with other descriptions.

A *seashore northward* (of the land southward) fits the east sea extending west to the neck of land – matching the north coast of Honduras into the Izabal Basin. (Fig. 15: index map for full seashore northward) And this fits the neck of land being in the Motagua Fault Zone.

To retreat along by *the seashore northward* the Nephite decoys could go east or west in drawing the Lamanites after them. But their goal was Bountiful in the neck of land to the west. Alma 52:19-36

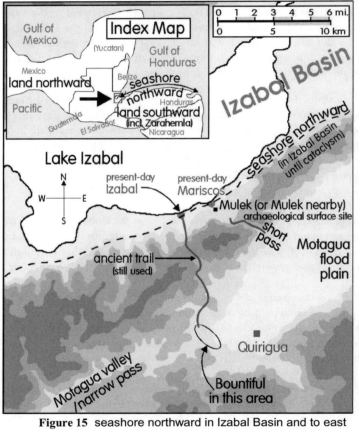

Figure 15 seashore northward in Izabal Basin and to east

Summary: The typesetter's punctuation doesn't fit the geologic evidence. Some may think that if the Book of Mormon is true there would be no errors. But the Book of Mormon in its preface says, about itself, that "if there are faults they are the mistakes of men." (Even the Bible has faults, otherwise there would not be the various translations that try to make it clearer.)

Joseph Smith was away at the time the Book of Mormon was printed and had turned supervision over to his brother Hyrum who had no reason to doubt the printer's punctuation.

Church History in the Fulness of Times, p. 64

With geology showing that the neck of land in the Motagua Fault Zone, the coast in the Izabal Basin and north coast of Honduras undoubtedly fit as the *seashore northward*. (index map, Fig. 15)

RIVER SIDON: The Sidon was not changed in the cataclysm, or but little, for it is mentioned in relation to the (local) land of Zarahemla later as it was before the event took place. (Alma 2:15; Mormon 1:10) It was a rather short river. This is seen in the escape of the prophet Alma and his people from a wicked king in a Nephite colony in the Lamanite land of Nephi, and in *the most capital parts of the land*.

Alma: His escape started in the borders of the land Nephi. He first fled 8 days into the wilderness to settle and build in a place he called Helam. (Fig. 16) It was then taken over by Lamanites as a Lamanite land and Alma and his people put into bondage. Years later, with divine help, they fled 13 days to the city of Zarahemla.

Mosiah 18:31-43;
23:1-5;24:2-25

It has been assumed that he went north for the 8 and 13 days to Zarahemla – a total of 21 days – with Helam on that route. But the Nephites in the colony, including Alma at the time, did not know the way to Zarahemla although they of course knew the general direction

50   Appendix

was north. (Mosiah 8:7, 8) Later Helam is mentioned along with other Lamanite lands. (Alma 24:1) Since these lands were south of the strip of wilderness that bordered the land of Zarahemla, Helam was south of that border too.

The west wilderness is called *the wilderness side* as if *wilderness* is the west wilderness unless stated otherwise. (Alma 8:3-6; 16:2; 22:28) This implies Alma went west when he escaped into the wilderness. Therefore, he did not go north to Helam but west on the Lamanite side of the narrow strip of wilderness that was the border with Zarahemla, until he reached Helam. (Fig. 12, p. 45) Then later, under divine guidance, he angled northeast to Zarahemla.

Besides, if he was going north to Zarahemla, why settle and build and till the ground at Helam? (Mosiah

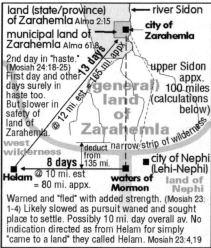

land (state/province) of Zarahemla Alma 2:15
municipal land of Zarahemla Alma 61:8
━━ river Sidon
city of Zarahemla

2nd day in "haste." (Mosiah 24:18-25) First day and other days surely in haste too. But slower in safety of land of Zarahemla.

upper Sidon appx. 100 miles (calculations below)

general land of Zarahemla

west wilderness

↑ deduct narrow strip from 135 mi.

land of Nephi

8 days ↓135 mi.

■ city of Nephi (Lehi-Nephi)

Helam @ 10 mi. est = 80 mi. appx.

waters of Mormon

land of Nephi

Warned and "fled" with added strength. (Mosiah 23: 1-4) Likely slowed as pursuit waned and sought place to settle. Possibly 10 mi. day overall av. No indication directed as from Helam for simply "came to a land" they called Helam. Mosiah 23:4,19

Diagonal course (hypotenuse) 156 mi.
  156 x 156 = 24,336
  - 80 x 80 = 6,400
  difference 17,936 and √17,936 = appx. 135 mi.
    Thus, headwaters to Zarahemla would be about
    135 miles less evidently short distance from
    latitudes of Mormon and Helam to headwaters
    - city Nephi near strip of wilderness (Mosiah 7:6,10)
    - Mormon likely near Nephi, for Alma went "among
      the people" yet to Mormon to teach (Alma 18:1-8)
    - suggests about 35 mi. max. to headwaters
Note: Waters of Mormon in borders of land of Nephi. (Mos. 18:4,5) Alma went west into wilderness so these borders were between land of Nephi and wilderness. - "The land, or the city, of Zarahemla" (Alma 61:8) indicates municipal land aound the city of Zarahemla where king Mosiah "did also receive" Alma. (Mosiah 24:20-25) To "also" be received by Mosiah, Alma had to first be received by others along the way in general land of Zarahemla. So *land of Zarahemla* where Mosiah received Alma was *municipal* or *state* land of Zarahemla. Mosiah could come from city to meet Alma and 13 days ended a little short of the city. But either way,13 days was essentially the same as to the city.

Figure 16 Alma and upper Sidon

23:5,19) This shows he just wanted to take his people where they could live in peace. And again, he did not know the way to Zarahemla until guided by God in escaping from Helam a number of years later.

Mosiah 8:7; 24:17

With geometry, as shown in Figure 16, we begin to see the length of the Sidon by these two diverging distances: 8 and 13 days, by first calculating its length from its head to Zarahemla. East or west, the geometry is the same. (that is, *general* east or west, even such as northeast or southwest.) The idea that he went north for 21 days does not fit his stay in Helam.

Note: Alma fled into the wilderness from the waters of Mormon "in the borders of the land." (Mosiah 18:4; 23:3) Since Helam was south of the border between the lands of Zarahemla and Nephi as noted above, this shows the wilderness he entered was not the narrow strip of wilderness which marked the border between Zarahemla and Nephi at this time. (Alma 22:27) The daily travel for Alma and his people would likely be 10-15 miles a day. Mosiah 24:18 Various travel ref.

Geometry suggests the city of Zarahemla was100 miles or so north of the Sidon's head. Alma's route would weave of course, according to the terrain. Point-to-point distances would be somewhat less than shown. (shown straight in Figure 16 to only represent travel time)

"The most capital parts of the land:" These "parts" were north of the city Zarahemla and help show the Sidon was a rather short river.

Helaman 1:27, 28

The most capital parts of any country are smaller than that overall land, for that is where government and commerce began with initial settlement. (few exceptions) For instance the *most capital parts* of the United States are in the northeast, which includes Washington D.C. and New York City. This region is much smaller than the rest of the U.S. but has the major centers of government and commerce.

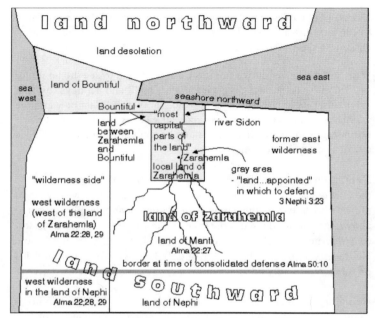

Figure 17 contracted defense in "appointed" land

The term, *the most capital parts of the land,* is used when invading
Lamanites took the city of Zarahemla and set out to take Bountiful.
(Ibid) (Fig. 17) The city of Bountiful was important since it defended
the narrow pass that led into the land northward. (Alma 52:9) So
context indicates *the most capital parts of the land* lay between these
two cities, as people and commerce are often strung out and clustered
between major cities even today.

Also, at one point the Nephites abandoned most of their land to con-
solidate for defense. The region "appointed" was "the land of Zarahemla, and...between the land Zarahemla and the land Bountiful" and

the land Bountiful itself. (the Bountiful-Desolation border was the northern limit) This would be the 'state' of Zarahemla, not the overall land Zarahemla.

They built "exceedingly great" defenses in a year's time to defend the region. Such building in such a short time indicates the region was relatively small. 3 Nephi 3:14,22,23; 4:1

The *most capital parts* of the land were in the *land appointed*, for they lay between the cities of Zarahemla and Bountiful which were in the land appointed. These two terms show a much smaller region north of the city Zarahemla.

That is, with *most capital parts* of a land being relatively small, and the *land appointed* being small enough to defend, it follows that the Sidon north of Zarahemla was notably shorter, for the distance across the smaller *capital/appointed* land to the sea would be shorter than from its head in the south where the land area would be greater.

The Ulúa river system (Fig. 7, p. 25) is only about 125 miles long and empties close to the Motagua Fault Zone that fits the site of the narrow neck of land. Santana, that fits as the site of Zarahemla beside the Ulúa, is about 90 miles from its headwaters and 35 miles from the Gulf of Honduras. (map, p. 83) The length of the Ulúa and the total geologic/geographic setting fits the Ulúa being the Sidon.

RUINS: It has been said that all early people came to the Americas from Asia by way of a land bridge that joined the two continents when the sea level was lower. And these people were ancestors of those who built the great structures in South and Central America and Mexico that are now in ruin. Now it is realized there were voyages to the Americas in ancient times although typically thought to have been by chance.

Whether by chance or exploring as with Lief Erickson probing along the northern east coast of North America or otherwise, this shows early ability to cross seas as told in the Book of Mormon. To whatever degree each mode of migration was used in the Americas' ancient settlement, the ruins testify of extensive cultures.

Members of The Church of Jesus Christ of Latter-day Saints see these ruins as evidence of the people of the Book of Mormon. But the cultures who built them, such as the Maya, often built later structures over earlier ones. (e.g. *Mysteries of the Ancient Americas*, p. 151, 152) So most ruins were built later and cover structures built in Book of Mormon times – but built by various peoples as discussed below.

Lamanites in the land northward:

> ...the Nephites had inhabited the land Bountiful...and... hemmed in the Lamanites on the south, that...**they should have no more possession on the north**, that they might not overrun the land northward. Alma 22:33; emphasis added

For the Lamanites to possibly gain *"more* possession on the north," (in the land northward) they already had to have *some possession* there. For this to be, Lamanites had to have made their way there earlier. Then, when Nephites moved into Bountiful, this would separate these Lamanites from Lamanites in the land southward.

Later, Nephites colonized in the land northward. Since Lamanites were there first and there is no indication of conflict at this time, evidently there was an accommodation with them for the Nephites to settle there. (Alma 63:4; Helaman 3:3-5) Only later do we know of warfare between them in the land northward. e.g. Mormon 4:7

Book of Mormon structures: The Nephites built with wood in the land southward. But they used cement in the land northward because there was a lack of timber caused by an earlier people called *Jaredites* who likely correlate as the ancient people archaeologists call *Olmecs*. Jarom 8; Al. 53:4; Helaman 3:6-10

Cement originally meant *mortar*. (*Webster*) Most ruins in Mesoamerica, which use cement, are north of the Motagua Fault Zone where there is a lot of limestone and clay to make cement. (The Yucatan, for instance, has been described as a "limestone shelf.")

The Ulúa valley of Honduras is an example where wood was used south of the Motagua Fault Zone, as the Book of Mormon indicates for the land southward. "The material used (south of Motagua) was less durable than stone and probably consisted of adobe and wood."
                    G. B. Gordon, *Researches in the Oloa* (sic) *Valley*, 1898, p.38
The only stone mentioned in the land southward was in fortifications. (Alma 48:8) These would be long overgrown. Wooden structures would not last in the Central American climate so there would likely be no ruins in the land southward from Book of Mormon times. (That is, south of the Motagua Fault Zone.)

The Nephites shipped timber to the land northward. (Helaman.3:6-10) This also indicates wood was their traditional building material. It would not last in the humid and lush climate just north of the Motagua Fault Zone either.

Indian **structures:** Some stone structures were built south of the Motagua Fault Zone and in the Zone where suitable stone and material for cement extended south. Even if the Nephites used some stone here too, perishable wood was their hallmark. The location of ruins fits the neck of land being in the Motagua Fault Zone for most ruins are north of it. (Fig. 18, next page)

Although most ruins are from after Book of Mormon times, they

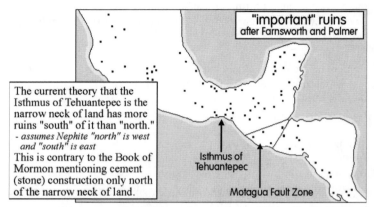

Figure 18 distribution of major ruins in Mesoamerica

show where materials for cement were available. That is, mainly
north of the Motagua Fault Zone, as the Book of Mormon has cement
north of the neck of land.

"Children of the land:" The Book of Mormon does not account for
all people in ancient America. It names those it tells of from the
present-day Middle (Near) East – Nephites, Lamanites, the people of
Zarahemla, and Jaredites. And it tells of "children of the land" in the
Americas. (Ether 2:10; see Genesis 23:7) It uses this term for the people in
Canaan when Israel came in there. (1 Nephi 17:32) This implies it meant
the same in the Americas; (indigenous) people were already there
when Book of Mormon peoples arrived. So there would be no dis-
agreement between the Book of Mormon and people having been in
the Americas for much longer than the Book of Mormon period.

The Nephites grouped all who were not *Nephite* as *Lamanite*. (e.g.
Mormon 1:9) This would include indigenous people. An LDS scholar

shows that not all people in the land northward chose to join in (Jaredite) civil war to die, nor chose to come to the land southward with the people of Zarahemla. (so-called *Mulekites*) (Nibley) And there were actual Lamanites. So the Nephites were greatly outnumbered in the north as south. Jarom vs. 6; Mosiah 25:3; 2 Nephi 5:21; 1 Nephi 12:20-23

For about 2700 years in the land northward, at least as early as the Jaredites/Olmecs, the *Indians* in a mix of indigenous, Jaredites, Mulekites, and Lamanites, built grand structures. The Nephites built houses of cement when they first went there. They are mentioned with tents. (Helaman 3:6-9) This implies a pioneer stage with temporary houses. (*Daub and wattle*: cement coating on a wicker framework.)

But even if the Nephites built structures such as pyramids, extensive building north of the Motagua Fault Zone was initiated long before the Nephites' time and continued long after. And if the Nephites built such structures, none have been identified as different than others for archaeologists to consider them as anything but *Indian* anyway.

Most ruins being north of the Motagua Fault Zone fits the Book of Mormon placing cement and the greatest population north of the neck of land. (Helaman 3:9; Mormon1:6 – 1830 edition, p.519 To go to Zarahemla, Mormon's father left the land northward, it *"having become* covered with buildings, and the people were...numerous almost...as...the sand of the sea.") And this fits geology placing the neck of land in the Moragua Fault Zone.

NARROW STRIP OF WILDERNESS AND LATER BORDER:
The first border between Nephites and Lamanites was a narrow strip of wilderness. *Wilderness* is "an uncultivated, uninhabited region." (Webster) It is not defined by the nature of the land but whether settled or not. It does not mean mountains or some other feature of the land.

A *strip of wilderness* implies a no-man's-land as typical with nations that border each other and are often at war. This boundary ran "from the sea east ...to the sea west, and round about." Alma 22:27

In contrast to "round about," the Nephites later set defenses on a "straight course from the east sea to the west." (Alma 50:8-10) This would not be like a ruler, but like a sailing ship on a *straight* or direct course does not go in a straight line but tacks with the wind, terrain varies too. So this "straight" border would deviate with the land.

The west sea is not stated with this new border but as the narrow strip of wilderness was sea to sea, it would be likewise with this border for the enemy could go around its inland end if it ended inland. The prophet who wrote this evidently saw it as redundant to say *sea* twice in this context. (see p. 70 for more about defenses and redundancy)

From ancient to modern times rivers and the nature of terrain have been used in defenses. And there are many rivers in Mesoamerica.

With the new border the Nephites sent "spies out round about" and the Lamanites also sent "spies round about." (Alma 56:22; 58:14) Nephite defences would surely include rivers in front of these defences as barriers to the enemy. Spies operating here imply another no-man's-land; likely on the Lamanite side of a river

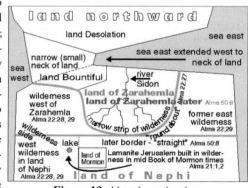

Figure 19 old and new borders

border and certainly in gaps between the rivers as noted below.

A river draining to the Gulf of Honduras and one to the Pacific align
sea to sea with other rivers and tributaries. This alignment suggests
a line from sea to sea but leaves three gaps in the west. (Fig. 20)

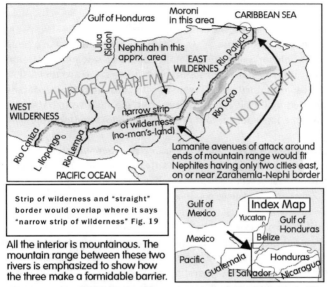

Figure 20 later "straight" border - compare Fig. 19

The Book of Mormon tells of cities in the west linked with this boundary. This implies extra defenses here which fortified cities in or near
these gaps could provide. They ended up being taken but their presence in spite of their failure is consistent with the gaps. Alma 56:14, 25

These rivers and tributaries align south of the source of the Ulúa, as the strip of wilderness ran sea to sea south of the Sidon's head. (Alma 22:27) These rivers could hopefully be barriers to invasion, particularly in the east where a mountain range and another river add more barriers. But this ultimately failed, likely due to its length, overpowering number of Lamanites, and Nephite unrighteousness. Mormon 1:16; 2:3

Comments: As noted, the river on the east coast does not empty eastward into the sea but into the Gulf of Honduras which is an extension of the Caribbean Sea, which matches as the east sea. This alignment of rivers still fits a border running from the west sea to the east sea – to the seashore northward formed by the east sea. So the defensive line formed by the rivers would run from the sea east to the sea west, marking the later border and providing sea-to-sea defense.

HILL CUMORAH: The hill Cumorah, where the Lamanites defeated the Nephites in their final battle, was in the land northward in a "land of many waters" that was "an exceedingly great distance" from Zarahemla. Mormon 6:4; Helaman 3:3,4

The hill in New York state called *Cumorah* where Moroni buried the plates, is not the original Cumorah. Early LDS Church members presumed it was since Moroni buried the plates here. (They overlooked Moroni travelling many years in order to reach it.) Geology points only to Latin America as the Book of Mormon scene. Moroni had the years to journey from Mesoamerica to New York state after the destruction of his people. Moroni 1:3; footnote – span of years

CORRELATION: On Mexico's Gulf coast there is an area laced with lakes, rivers, and lagoons. (Fig. 21) In this region is the massive hill, *Cerro Vigia,* that fits the location and conditions likely for Cumorah.
David A. Palmer, *In Search of Cumorah*, p. 96-101

As noted, Cumorah was an exceeding great distance from Zarahemla.

Exceeding means "surpassing; extraordinary; extreme." (Webster) This
distance is stated in connection with Nephites leaving Zarahemla to
colonize in the land northward.   Helaman 3:3,4

Since elements
can combine as
Zurahuma in
the Sula/Zura
valley as an
echo of *Zara-*
hemla, this val-
ley fits as the
place to mea-
sure the dis-
tance from. (p.
30) This would
be an *exceed-*
ing great dist-
ance for it far

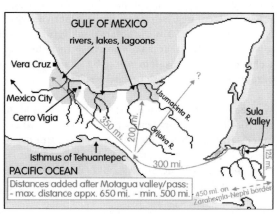

Figure 21

exceeds what would surely be the Nephites' normal sphere of activity
in the Sidon/Uluá watershed. This great distance from Zurahuma and
several factors not covered here show Cerro Vigia to likely be the
actual hill Cumorah. Or it could be one of other large nearby hills.

Yet Cerro Vigia and its environs have all the attributes but they are
not gone into in this outline. Ironically, this hill is the one that most
students of the subject say is Cumorah yet they come to their conclusion for reasons inconsistent with the Book of Mormon account.

BIBLE PROPHECIES: Isaiah chapter 29 The prophet Isaiah
calls Jerusalem

          Ariel, the city [where] David dwelt!...
And adds the following:

add ye year to year; let them kill sacrifices. Yet I will
distress Ariel...and **it shall be unto me as Ariel**.

Isaiah 29:1,2 emphasis added

Jerusalem is *Ariel* and compared to another *Ariel* which Mormons
say is the Nephite civilization in the Americas which was destroyed.
On the other hand, Bible scholars think Jerusalem is being compared
to itself here. But that makes no sense since there is no indication of
a change when Jerusalem would be in a different condition to compare its former self with its later self.

We see that Ariel (Jerusalem) will be distressed in spite of offering
sacrifices. And Jerusalem is referred to as *it* when compared to the
other *Ariel* which will also be distressed. But the other Ariel is addressed directly. That is, the first Ariel, Jerusalem, is spoken of in the
third person. But the other Ariel is in the *second person* since it is
addressed directly.

This indicates two *Ariels* in addition to the incongruity of comparing
Jerusalem to itself. And the forces to strike *Ariel* show there are two.

But first, in speaking to the other Ariel, Isaiah says,

thou shalt be brought down, [and] shalt speak out of the
ground, and thy speech shall be low out of the dust, and thy
voice shall be, as of one that hath a familiar spirit, out of
the ground, and thy speech shall whisper out of the dust.

Isaiah 29:4

The term "familiar spirit" is used here relative to the other Ariel. In
the ancient Middle (Near) East, one who had a *familiar spirit* sup-
posedly communicated with the dead. In the West this is a supposed
medium between living and dead. In the ancient Middle East, in
their pretense of communicating with the dead, mediums faked a
whispering voice, trying to make it seem to be from out of the
ground – akin to ventriloquism.

Critics of the Book of Mormon say this scripture refers to mediums. But Isaiah does not say a medium is involved. Rather, he says the speech of this other Ariel, which is "brought down," would come from the ground "**as** of one that hath a familiar spirit." That is, as if a person claiming a familiar spirit was involved. This is shown more clearly in translations other than the King James' that say "*like* those that had familiar spirits."   e.g. Thomas Scott, *The Holy Bible with Commentary*, p. 4; emphasis added

The other Ariel, speaking "out of the ground," fits the Book of Mormon plates being buried in the ground and coming forth to "speak" of this nation that was brought down. In speaking *to* the other Ariel, (note the second person form) Isaiah says,

> Thou shalt be visited of the LORD of hosts with thunder, and with earthquake, and great noise, with storm and tempest, and the flame of devouring fire. Isaiah 29:6

This is described as if one event, when all these forces would be unleashed. There is no record of Jerusalem being assailed by these atmospheric phenomena, "great noise, with storm and tempest," and by earthquake and fire in one event. It experienced earthquake when Christ was crucified and fire when it was taken by Babylon and later by Rome. But both of these forces were not involved together in these or any other events. And again, neither did Jerusalem endure "great noise, with storm and tempest" together or alone.

Bible scholars take this description of forces as a simile for the advance of the Assyrians on Jerusalem as, "*like* thunders, earthquakes, storms, and tempests." (e.g. Scott, p. 4) But this is inconsistent, for the Assyrian advance failed due to plague in their camp and they never reached Jerusalem. Compare this with the Book of Mormon saying,

> And it came to pass in the thirty and fourth year...there arose a great storm, such an one as never had been known in all the land.

> And there was also a great and terrible tempest; and there
> was terrible thunder, insomuch that it did shake the whole
> earth as if it was about to divide asunder.
>
> And there were exceedingly sharp lightnings, such as never
> had been known in all the land.
>
> And the city of Zarahemla did take fire. 3 Nephi 8:5-8

Then Isaiah says more about this nation and foretells spiritual drow-
siness and implies an awakening through a book that is "delivered."

> For the LORD hath poured out upon you the spirit of deep
> sleep...
>
> And the vision of all is become unto you as the words of a
> book that is sealed, which [men] deliver to one that is
> learned, saying, Read this, I pray thee: and he saith, I
> cannot; for it [is] sealed:
>
> And the book is delivered to him that is not learned, saying,
> Read this, I pray thee: and he saith, I am not learned.
>
> Isaiah 29:10-12

Only one third of the Book of Mormon could be translated for the
rest of it was sealed. The original plates that comprised the Book of
Mormon were delivered by an angel to the young Joseph Smith, who
was a farmer's son with very little education who acknowledged his
lack of learning.

A neighboring farmer, Martin Harris, mortgaged his farm to pay for
publication of the Book of Mormon. In making this decision he
wanted verification that what Joseph claimed about the book was
true. So Joseph copied some characters from the plates on a sheet of
paper for him, with their translation. Then, with a friend, Martin took
these to Professor Charles Anthon in New York City who was an
expert in ancient languages.

Martin said Prof. Anthon gave him a certificate, saying these characters and translation were authentic. Then Prof. Anthon asked where they came from and when Martin said they came from a book of gold plates delivered by an angel, Prof. Anthon asked for the certificate back. Martin thought he was going to add something to it but instead tore it up, saying there was no such thing as ministering angels now. Yet he said to bring the plates to him and he would translate them.

Then Martin told Prof. Anthon that most of the plates were sealed and he replied, "I cannot read a sealed book." (*History of the Church in the Fulness of Times*, p. 46) But even without the certificate Martin was satisfied by Prof. Anthon saying the characters were authentic and paid for publication of the Book of Mormon.

Analysis: Prof. Anthon was not asked to read the Book of Mormon plates, but asked to read "the words" of the book as delivered to him by "men:" Martin Harris and his friend fit Isaiah's word.

The degree of agreement with Isaiah is notable. That is, "the words" in Isaiah's statement would have to mean just some of the words, for if it meant all the words, that would mean the full book itself and the distinction between the *words of the book* and *the book* itself would be meaningless. This distinction between words of the book delivered by men, and the book itself to the unlearned is fulfilled in Prof. Anthon and Joseph Smith.

A marvellous work: After telling of the words and book, Isaiah
says: Wherefore the Lord said, Forasmuch as this people...have
             removed their heart far from me...

             Therefore, behold, I will proceed to do a marvellous work
             among this people, [even] a marvellous work and a wonder:
             for the wisdom of their wise [men] shall perish, and the
             understanding of their prudent [men] shall be hid.

                                                                   Isaiah 29:13, 14

A "marvellous work and a wonder" would come forth. The description fits the Book of Mormon which has awakened many to the gospel of Jesus Christ and brought futility to those who try to explain it away.

> And in that day shall the deaf hear the words of the book, and the eyes of the blind shall see out of obscurity, and out of darkness. Isaiah 29:18

Here Isaiah tells of the book overcoming spiritual deafness and blindness. (Isaiah 29:10) These things give the reason for the book he speaks of, which fits "the intent" of the Book of Mormon. (p. 6)

Ezekiel chapter 37: The Bible comes from the Jews, descendants of Judah, one of the sons of Jacob. (Israel) Another son was Joseph. The two of them are mentioned when the Lord told Ezekiel,

> Moreover, thou son of man, take thee one stick, and write upon it, For Judah...then take another stick, and write upon it, For Joseph...
>
> And join them one to another into one stick; and they shall become one in thine hand.
>
> And when...thy people shall [ask]...shew us what thou meanest by these?
>
> Say unto them, Thus saith the Lord God; Behold, I will take the stick of Joseph...and...the stick of Judah...and they shall be one in mine hand. Ezekiel 37:16-19

The full passage mentions Joseph's part being achieved through Ephraim, one of his two sons, who had the birthright. (Genesis 48:1-20) As noted on page one of this booklet, the people who wrote the Book of Mormon were descendants of Joseph. Their ancestry includes both of Joseph's sons but the Ephriam heritage has precedence.

In this passage God tells Ezekiel to make a visual aid. That is, take two sticks and write on them for Judah and for Joseph, to hold in his hand as tokens of two sticks God would hold as one in His hand. But what is meant by a *stick* in this context?

Without going into the detail since this is only an outline, we find that the Hebrew word translated as "stick" is translated this way 14 times and as *wood* 249 times. This shows its overriding meaning to be wood. But how could Ezekiel write on wood?

Anciently recesses were carved into wooden tablets and filled with wax to incise temporary writing with a stylus. They were used separately or tied and hinged together. (Fig. 22) These tablets would correlate as the wood or "sticks" Ezekiel mentions. (As a matter of interest: In the movie *Ben Hur*, the Arab sheik taking bets on the chariot race wrote on wax-filled tablets.)

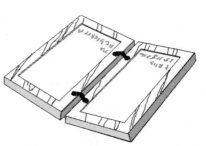

Figure 22

They would "become one" in Ezekiel's hand – symbolic of the Lord joining the writing of Judah and Joseph (Ephraim) as one in His hand. That is, the Bible from Judah and the Book of Mormon from Joseph would be joined as one in the Lord's hand. The Church of Jesus Christ of Latter-day Saints, claiming divine guidance, has joined these two together in providing the Word of God.

Of course they are not sticks as Ezekiel had. *Stick* is a metaphor when it comes to the real thing. Besides, an original term can be applied to something although its nature has changed. The original description can endure. For example, golf woods are now metal.

Summary: The writings of Old testament prophets usually baffle most readers. But sometimes their statements stand out clearly. For instance, when Isaiah writes, "For unto us a child is born, unto us a son is given....The Prince of Peace," we see this is a clear statement about the birth of Christ. (Isaiah 9:6) Likewise, in the body of Isaiah's and Ezekiel's writings, these prophecies about a book and about writing stand out and fit the Book of Mormon.

NECK OF LAND, NARROW? As the geology of the Motagua Fault Zone shows, the Izabal Basin was lower before the cataclysm. This basin is formed by mountains, so when the sea (Gulf of Honduras) extended inland it formed a finger of the sea about 50 miles long and 15 miles wide. (see Fig. 20, p. 59 and map pp. 82-83) At this *place* the sea *divided* the land. But although the land is narrow from sea to sea compared to the land just north and south of it, the Zone seems rather wide for what we might expect for a narrow neck of land. How can this be reconciled?

Narrow: Since the neck of land lay between the seas east and west, it has been assumed that it ran north-south and was narrow between these seas. As noted, geology shows the narrow neck of land was in the Motagua Fault Zone, *but*, even with the sea extending into the Izabal Basin, it is not very narrow between the seas. (Fig. 21, p. 61) So what does *narrow* mean here in Nephite terms?

Evident answer: (Fig. 23) In exploring the land of Zarahemla after they arrived (whether guided or not by the people of Zarahemla who were there first and they united with) the Nephites would have come to the neck of land from the south via the valley of the river Sidon. (Omni vs.13,14) The surrounding land was mountainous.

> Alma 2:15; 3 Nephi 2:9,17;
> 3:17,20,23; 4:1

With the mountains to the east and west hindering travel, the logical route to the north would be the Sidon valley to the coast, and west to the neck of land. (The neck of land is shown angled to the southwest since the Motagua Fault Zone, which fits the geology for the narrow neck of land is at this approximate angle.)

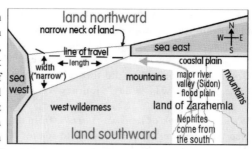

Figure 23 orientation of narrow neck o f land

The Motagua Fault Zone lies in an east-west direction. *It is narrow from north to south – as viewed from the east.* This alignment fits the geology and indications the Nephites would come north in the Sidon valley and then west. They would also come to the narrow pass in the neck of land. The pass also lay east-west in the neck of land as does the Motagua valley in the Motagua Fault Zone. (Fig. 4, p. 14)

This orientation from the east can account for the neck of land being narrow or small from the Nephites' viewpoint. They still called it this where it was wider to the west at the Pacific. (As things often retain original names even when a new aspect is found. e.g. [American] Indians are still called *Indians* though they have nothing to do with India.) Alma 63:5

This analysis agrees with the geology that puts the neck of land in the Motagua Fault Zone and being narrow from the Nephites' likely perspective. Still, it was narrow from sea to sea compared to the land north and south of the Motagua Fault Zone. So either view could fit.

DEFENCES AND NECK OF LAND: The neck of land and the land Bountiful are both described in the same location, between the lands northward and southward. So what was their relationship? (Alma 22:32-34) It is seen when the Nephites were "driven...into the land Bountiful" where "they did fortify"on a line "from the west sea to the east." This was "a day's journey for a Nephite." Helaman 4:6,7

We saw the neck of land was *narrow* from north to south, yet it was also the narrowest place from sea to sea for it was "the place where the sea divide(d) the land." (Ether 10:20) The sea would have to cut into the land to divide it, making it narrowest from the end of this 'cut' to the opposite (west) sea. (Fig. 12, p. 46; Fig. 3, p. 13) It is only logical that the Nephites would defend where they could set the shortest line after driven "into" Bountiful. Thus they would surely set it where the sea cut into the land; where it was narrowest *sea to sea*.

So to be precise about the neck of land and Bountiful being in the same place, the neck of land had to be in the land Bountiful and the land Bountiful was not somehow in the neck of land. (Fig. 19, p. 58)

Objections: Because this text says *sea* only once, it has been thought that this line ran from one sea to an inland point where terrain was too rugged for the Lamanites to skirt around it. But an ancient military axiom says, "Where an animal can go, a man can follow. And where a man can follow, an army can pass."

In telling of this line it would be redundant to say *sea* twice, like saying, "I went to the first house and then to the second house." We would likely say "I went to the first house and then to the second." We wouldn't say *house* a second time. Likewise, context indicates this defensive line was sea to sea.

This is supported by an instance where the Book of Mormon *is* redundant by mentioning both seas for a line that ran sea to sea. That is, the narrow strip of wilderness ran "from the sea east...to the sea west." (Alma 22:27) Likewise, the line in the neck of land would also have to be from sea to sea so a Lamanite army could not "pass."

From place to place: Defenses need a trail or road for movement to defend anywhere along its length whether in ancient or modern times, and for communication. The Nephites had horses. (More about this later to substantiate the claim.) So a courier on relays of horses could carry messages as with other ancient peoples. (an example follows) So "a Nephite" rider/courier on a road or trail would have advantage over a Lamanite going parallel in the wilderness.

Thus, "a day's journey for a Nephite" and not just "a day's journey."

An example: In 1588 the Spanish were expected to attempt an invasion of England so the English prepared a sequence of bon fires running inland from the coast that were lit to warn the country when the ships of the Spanish armada was seen approaching. This was followed by details carried inland by messengers on horseback.

                    Burt Hirschfield, *The Spanish Armada*, p. 88, 119

There is no mention of relays of horses but this makes the point that a rider in early times was needed to relay detailed information.

As for the Nephites, the *Valle de Las Vacas* runs from the Motagua valley to the Pacific, with the two valleys forming a corridor from sea to sea in which a defensive line could be set. (Fig. 25, p. 78)

There is an ancient trail, still used, from the Motagua valley into the Izabal Basin, with mounds covering structures beside it where it ends in the basin. It fits as the east end of a trail connecting defenses from sea to sea. The buried structures indicate the importance of this end of the trail, which also fits as the place where the Lamanites were repelled in the borders of Bountiful when they invaded along the east coast. (Cities taken had "fortifications," so this place in the borders of Bountiful was likely better fortified to not be taken.) Alma 51:22-31

Since this was a military situation a civilian could not just take a walk along the line nor a soldier do so. But a soldier on assignment such as a courier could. But this defensive line in the Motagua Fault Zone context would be about 150 miles long, so horses would be the only means for "a Nephite" to go that distance in a day.

Some suggest "a Nephite" was a runner but only genetically exceptional individuals have the capacity to run this far this fast. Besides, a Nephite would not have much advantage over a Lamanite running the same distance in the wilderness, and "a Nephite" is more inclusive for surely any Nephite soldier could learn to ride such a distance.

Of course it is believed that horses in the Americas had gone extinct and new stock came with the Spanish. But one authority speaks of their "*apparent* disappearance." (Stock, *Rancho La Brea*, p. 43 Emphasis added) And finds have been made that show horses were present with man before the Spanish came. (horse bones with artifacts)

Cited by Sorenson, *An American Setting for the Book of Mormon*, p. 295, 395

But another archaeologist states that the sequence for these bones is "uncertain" and says there is no art representing horses in support of horses being known of by the Indians. (And presumably by the Nephites.)   Deanne Matheny, in *New Approaches to the Book of Mormon*, p. 30

Quetzalcoatl: As for no art, a carved plaque in a temple wall at Chichen Itza in the Yucatan made about 500 years before the Spanish came, shows a horse with rider. It is crude by our standards but instructive. (Fig. 24) It is the central plaque of dozens, indicating it was the main subject.

Figure 24: The photograph shown here was taken in the early 1970s. Another photograph in 1992 was worse because of more erosion.

The eroding was bad enough circa 1970 but that photograph is the better one. So it has been somewhat computer defined due to poor definition. (lower photo) This could be taken further but this is enough to suitably clarify the image and going further might seem to be manipulating it.

Due to the erosion some have thought there is only one human figure and one animal such as a peccary or tapir, pig-like animals similar to a large pig in size. (e.g. Sorenson, pers. comm.; *Webster* for "pig-like") Others have seen the animal as horse-sized with a figure standing beside it without mentioning a figure seated on the animal. (e.g. Hunter, *Archaeology and the Book of Mormon*, p. 5, 6) But there seem to be two animals, one smaller and overlapping the other. And the enhancement shows two men – one with a figurative head, mounted, and one walking alongside. The relative size of the man walking shows this animal or animals to be the size of a horse.

I asked a guide at Chichen Itza what this animal is and he said "It looks like a horse but can't be because horses were extinct before the Spanish came." Then I asked him, "How do you account for it?" He said, "We can't." I asked him who the seated figure on the animal epresents. He said, "Quetzalcoatl." (The symbolic head of this figure is the feathered serpent that represents Quetzalcoatl.) The guide said the shape coming from Quetzelcoatl's mouth is a jaguar. (more about this shortly) When asked about the element in the lower right corner he said it represents corn leaves.

We saw evidence that Quetzalcoatl is the Indians' cultural memory of Christ. In this carving we have Quetzalcoatl riding on an animal that looks like a horse. The Bible says Christ made his triumphal

eroded carving - Temple of the Plaques, Chichen Itza, Mexico
photo courtesy Ted E. Brewerton

computer defined to clarify figures & relative sizes: horses(s) & men
("Quetzalcoatl" seated on animal and man standing alongside)

Figure 24

entry into Jerusalem riding on "the foal of an ass." Its mother would have been with it for the disciples who got it "brought the ass, and the colt." Matthew 21:1-8; Luke 19:35

So there were two animals in the biblical account. As He rode into Jerusalem the people "cut down branches...and strawed them in the way." Matt. 21:8

In light of the indicators that Quetzalcoatl was the Indians' cultural memory of Christ, Quetzalcoatl riding is consistent with Christ riding into Jerusalem on a donkey's colt with its mother alongside although the carving suggests them promoted to a horse and colt. Whether one animal or two, this echoes Christ's entry into Jerusalem.

The man walking alongside the animal and Quetzalcoatl would be consistent with a disciple attending Christ as He rode. The man's extended leg indicates that he is indeed walking as the extended legs of Quetzalcoatl's mount shows it is too. The "corn leaves" seem too broad. They seem more like palm fronds as traditionally associated with Christ's entrance into Jerusalem. But whatever they are, they are foliage in Quetzalcoatl's path as he rides, just as "branches" were strewn in Christ's path as He rode into Jerusalem.

The supposed "jaguar" coming from Quetzalcoatl's mouth is a nebulous shape that seems more an attempt to represent a concept rather than a jaguar. This could fit as the Spirit or Word of God emanating from him. Except for the donkeys upgraded to horses, the subject of the carving – Quetzalcoatl riding an animal with foliage in his path, suggests Christ's 'triumphal entry' into Jerusalem.

The carving is consistent with the Book of Mormon saying Christ told the people in the Americas about His ministry in Jerusalem. But "not even a hundredth part" is recorded. (3 Ne. 15:14-23; 26:6) Therefore many details of His ministry in Judea are not given in the Book of Mormon, so not mentioning Christ's entry into Jerusalem does not disallow the story of his ride being handed down in the Americas.

This carving fits the context of the Book of Mormon. Neither Joseph Smith nor anyone else could produce this context and have the Indians support it hundreds of years in advance with a carving unknown in 1830 that appears very much to agree with this biblical account.

Animals: Names of known animals have been used for unknown animals such as when Europeans in North America first saw herds of bison and called them *buffalo*. So it is argued by some that sometimes familiar animal names in the Book of Mormon are for different animals, so a *horse* was not necessarily a horse. But here we have a pre-Spanish carving that appears to fit Christ's entry into Jerusalem.

With donkeys related to horses, the substitution of a horse and colt by descendants of Book of Mormon peoples, with only the tradition, is understandable. Or they could think a horse to be more fitting for Quetzalcoatl than a donkey. But regardless of the basis for this carving, horses in the carving show that pre-Spanish Indians had horses to know what they are, for judging by the size of these animals compared with the walking figure of a man, this is a horse. (or horses)

The essential thing is that an Indian carver in pre-Spanish times knew what a horse is like. Whether there were horses at hand or the carver had drawings in early books/codexes as reference, his carving, although crude, shows the horse was known by the Indians before the arrival of the Spanish and were ridden in that earlier time.

Either way, even this carving alone shows horses were present before the Spanish came and so they would have also been present earlier, in the Book of Mormon period. This brings us back to the indication that the one-day journey for *a Nephite* on the defensive line in Bountiful involved Nephite couriers riding relays of horses.

One-day journey: A rider using a series of horses, as with the Pony Express of the old west, could average 10 mph over distances up to 150 miles and even more. (*World Book Ency.,* 1964, v. P, p.583, 4) Ancient empires of the Middle East such as the Assyrian and Persian used riders on relays of horses to carry dispatches over long distances.

In the same way "a Nephite" courier using a succession of horses as mentioned, riding on a trail or road linking fortifications, could travel the 150 miles through the Valle de Vacas and Motagua Valley corridor in one day, whether it be a 24-hour day or less. His travel would be the length of the neck of land from sea to sea. (Fig. 25 - next page)

With Lehi's people coming from the Middle/Near East they could have known of relays of horses if they did not think of it independently. Either way, having horses would enable *a Nephite* to go 150 miles in a day on the defensive line in Bountiful. Such a line would be lengthy to defend but the Book of Mormon tells of two classes of military: "guards and armies." (Alma 22:33) This indicates guards along the line to warn of attack and soldiers to get there for defense. And how would guards alert the armies?

We saw the example with the Spanish armada. Even if the Nephites used signal fires, guards and armies would require couriers to transmit detailed information to officers for disposition of forces.

Couriers fit the Book of Mormon and any defensive line. The trench warfare of World War I used dispatch riders on motorcycles. By any means available in any age, forces need to transmit information. This would be the Nephites' need too. And they had horses which would be their fastest means; thus "a day's journey for a Nephite."

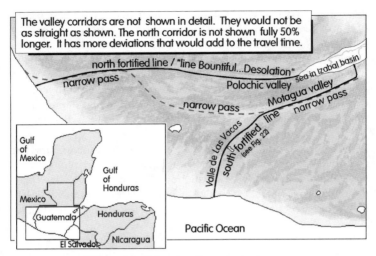

Figure 25 defensive lines and narrow pass

Note re. Fig. 25: There was also the "line Bountiful and the land Desolation, from the east to the west sea" when the Nephites occupied the land Bountiful for defensive reasons. (Alma 22:32, 33) The Bountiful-Desolation line was likely defensive for it is mentioned in the context of Nephite security and described in the same terms as the line on the south which is stated to be a defense. It was 50% longer and marked the north edge of the neck of land.

APOSTASY, CHURCHES, AND RESTORATION: This gets into delicate territory for there are many good people who look to their religious heritage with high regard. But the apostle Paul declared,

> the day of Christ (His Second Coming)...shall not come, except there come a falling away first. (*apostasy* in Greek text)
>
> 2 Thessalonians 2:1-4

This falling away came about with the death of the apostles and contention among leaders such as bishops, about doctrine and leadership. Among other biblical statements about this falling away, Paul said,

> in latter times some shall depart from the faith, giving heed to deceiving spirits, and...Forbidding to marry.

1 Timothy 4:1-3 – early Greek

"Forbidding to marry" could not apply to all who would "depart from the faith," for that would prevent birth of future generations. (Unless conceived immoraly, but this would not fit a church that claimed to be Christ's.) So it would have to apply to only some members, as required for the clergy of the Roman Catholic Church.

Other churches of 'historic Christianity' broke from the Roman Catholic in the Reformation period. Most were established to "reform," to become like the original church of Christ. And all of them, including the Roman Catholic, included many good people who have done many good things. But one further step was needed.

That is, the apostle Peter said there would a restoration when

> the times of refreshing shall come from the presence of the Lord; And he shall send Jesus Christ...Whom the heavens must receive until the times of restitution of all things, which God hath spoken by the mouth of all his holy prophets since the world began. Acts 3:19-21

After Christ's resurrection He was "received up into heaven." (Mark 16:19) And Peter said, as just cited, heaven must still "receive" Christ until the "restitution (restoration) of all things."

Since a thing cannot be reinstated unless it has been removed or lost, a restitution of "*all* things...spoken" by his prophets implies loss of His true doctrine with the death of the original apostles. Yet many stayed faithful to Christ without full knowledge of His gospel, even to joining in the Reformation with hope of finding more.

The prophet Amos said God "does nothing without revealing his plan to his servants the prophets." (Amos 3:7 Hebrew text) The restoration would need leadership for mankind as needed anciently, so Christ would surely raise up a prophet in that role. Since Joseph Smith was the one chosen to provide the Book of Mormon that fits as the book foretold by Isaiah and Ezekiel, he would fit as that prophet.

The non-Christian: This introduction to the need for restoration of the original gospel addresses Christians and nominal Christians. But most of the world is non-Christian so the Book of Mormon says

> ...the Lord doth grant unto all nations, of their own nation and tongue, to teach his word, yea, in wisdom, all that he seeth fit that they should have... Alma 29:8

That is, the Lord has provided all people a measure of truth through the religions they have until they can hear the fullness of the gospel, which adds to the truth they have. To this end, the Book of Mormon has "the intent that there should be no cause for unbelief among the children of men" regarding Christ. Helaman 14:28, 29

Belief in Him is belief in the Son of God who is God in his own right. (John 1:1; Mosiah 13:28) It is not belief in a man's word and theology which adherents can only claim is of God.

Question and deny: Some doubt and some deny there is God and demean faith in Him. But they have faith...in study of the earth's past by those who conclude it all came by chance! They have been taught to have faith that an immense number of chance events culminated in the many intricate systems that make a living body whether human or animal. And this is massively multiplied by the great number of species for each would have its own sequence of chance events.

If chance is the prime mover it follows that chance endowed our world with astounding assets: e.g. metals, minerals, petroleum – which just by 'chance' benefit mankind. (Imagine life without them.) And just by 'chance' we have the means to use them for millions of things from building skyscrapers to devising intricate computers, to travelling in ways that would astound earlier generations, and harnessing the unseen forces surrounding us such as shrinking the world with radio and TV waves and creating electrical power from sunlight.

All this, and the astounding brain to do it, evolved by chance?

The inexpressibly great number of chance events needed for life, and for these assets, and for the means to use them, to have just happened, do not fit *The Mathematics of Probability*. Rather, they testify of God who happens to be. (Without being sacrilegious: His existence is one marvellous happenstance rather than an impossible number of happenstances required by evolutionary theory.)

Some think that *if* God exists He would not allow the many travesties in the world. But if He intervened to prevent them from doing a thing, they would surely complain. They feel the right to do as they choose and this is the point. God allows them to choose, and all mankind also. Some choose to inflict travesties. Those who believe in God take comfort in knowing that later, if only in the life to come, justice will be served. And those who choose right will be rewarded.

For Christian and non-Christian, for those who deny or question the existence of God, the findings foretold present themselves as evidence of Christ to be honestly assessed. As a result they are objective evidence for the Book of Mormon since it tells of these things.

The challenge is to put aside preconceptions that hinder objectivity. The significance of the evidence is outlined on pages 1-8 and 37.

setting of
geologic evidence

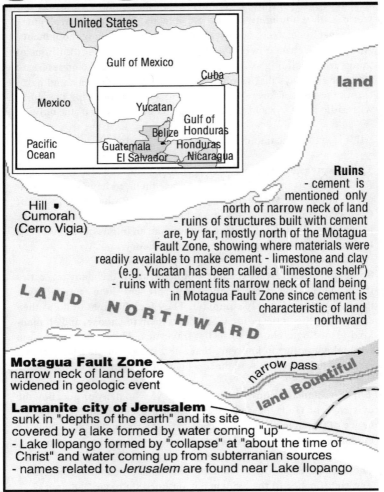

United States

Gulf of Mexico

Cuba

land

Mexico

Yucatan

Gulf of Honduras

Belize

Pacific Ocean

Guatemala

Honduras

El Salvador

Nicaragua

Hill • Cumorah (Cerro Vigia)

Ruins
- cement is mentioned only north of narrow neck of land
- ruins of structures built with cement are, by far, mostly north of the Motagua Fault Zone, showing where materials were readily available to make cement - limestone and clay (e.g. Yucatan has been called a "limestone shelf") - ruins with cement fits narrow neck of land being in Motagua Fault Zone since cement is characteristic of land northward

LAND NORTHWARD

narrow pass

land Bountiful

Motagua Fault Zone - narrow neck of land before widened in geologic event

Lamanite city of Jerusalem - sunk in "depths of the earth" and its site covered by a lake formed by water coming "up"
- Lake Ilopango formed by "collapse" at "about the time of Christ" and water coming up from subterranian sources
- names related to *Jerusalem* are found near Lake Ilopango

created at time of the Savior's death

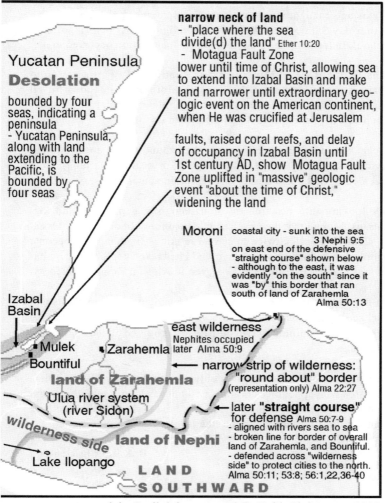

narrow neck of land
- "place where the sea divide(d) the land" Ether 10:20
- Motagua Fault Zone lower until time of Christ, allowing sea to extend into Izabal Basin and make land narrower until extraordinary geologic event on the American continent, when He was crucified at Jerusalem

faults, raised coral reefs, and delay of occupancy in Izabal Basin until 1st century AD, show Motagua Fault Zone uplifted in "massive" geologic event "about the time of Christ," widening the land

Yucatan Peninsula

Desolation

bounded by four seas, indicating a peninsula
- Yucatan Peninsula, along with land extending to the Pacific, is bounded by four seas

Moroni   coastal city - sunk into the sea
3 Nephi 9:5
on east end of the defensive "straight course" shown below
- although to the east, it was evidently "on the south" since it was "by" this border that ran south of land of Zarahemla
Alma 50:13

Izabal Basin

■ Mulek   ■ Zarahemla

east wilderness
Nephites occupied later Alma 50:9

Bountiful

land of Zarahemla

Ulua river system (river Sidon)

narrow strip of wilderness: "round about" border (representation only) Alma 22:27

wilderness side   **land of Nephi**

Lake Ilopango

later **"straight course"** for defense Alma 50:7-9
- aligned with rivers sea to sea
- broken line for border of overall land of Zarahemla, and Bountiful.
- defended across "wilderness side" to protect cities to the north. Alma 50:11; 53:8; 56:1,22,36-40

L A N D   S O U T H W A R D

About the Author

Years ago I taught in an early morning seminary program in which Latter-day Saint youth attend a daily religion class before going to school. In teaching the Book of Mormon a question occurred to me.

That is, the Book of Mormon offers a spiritual way for a person to learn it is true. But since the Book of Mormon is intended for all mankind, does it also offer a way for people in general who are not prepared to test it spiritually to also learn it is true?

I checked in the Book of Mormon and found that it does, through evidence of the great geologic disaster that struck its lands. So I decided to find out if the findings foretold actually exist.

By looking into research by archaeologists, geologists, and historians, I found that the physical evidence foretold does exist. I went to Central America twice to see these things firsthand. To become familiar with the disciplines involved I had taken geology and archaeology classes in getting a B.A. degree at Brigham Young University.

In the course of this research I have consulted with geologists and archaeologists since sources in both disciplines are involved in the research. The opinion of two of them are provided on the back of the title page.

I emphasize that this booklet is only an introduction. The complete research with appendices is almost 500 pages long. I plan to present much of it later. In the meantime I hope the material presented here opens a door for you to see that the Book of Mormon is authentic.

B. Keith Christensen